Pantheon
The Egyptians

Pantheon
The Egyptians

Robin Herne

MOON
BOOKS

Winchester, UK
Washington, USA

JOHN HUNT PUBLISHING

First published by Moon Books, 2021
Moon Books is an imprint of John Hunt Publishing Ltd., No. 3 East Street, Alresford
Hampshire SO24 9EE, UK
office@jhpbooks.net
www.johnhuntpublishing.com
www.moon-books.net

For distributor details and how to order please visit the 'Ordering' section on our website.

Text copyright: Robin Herne 2020

ISBN: 978 1 78535 504 2
978 1 78535 505 9 (ebook)
Library of Congress Control Number: 2019955387

A CIP catalogue record for this book is available from the British Library.

Design: Stuart Davies

UK: Printed and bound by CPI Group (UK) Ltd, Croydon, CR0 4YY
Printed in North America by CPI GPS partners

We operate a distinctive and ethical publishing philosophy in
all areas of our business, from our global network of authors to
production and worldwide distribution.

Contents

I would like to express my thanks to Trevor Greenfield for first suggesting the idea of this book. Thanks also go to Nick Ford and Jo Hutchings for their assistance with proofreading and some insightful input.

This book is dedicated to the memory of Gwynn, my elderly and adorable husky, who passed away as I came near to the end of the manuscript. I miss my little wolf more than I can say.

Finally, *dua* and thanks must go to Wepwawet, the Opener of the Ways, who has assisted in the writing of this book.

Foreword

This book is aimed at the person who has an interest in the beliefs and rituals of Ancient Egypt but has yet to put ideas into practice. It is hoped that there is enough detail to also appeal to the more experienced practitioner. The book interweaves history with theology, philosophy, ethics, a little mysticism, and some practical advice on how to engage with the deities and spirits of the ancient land.

The culture and achievements of Egypt have had a profound influence on Africa, Europe, and the New World. Not only has it permeated geographical boundaries but also shaped many religions, both monotheist and polytheist. For many this influence may be subtle to the point of invisibility, whilst others openly acknowledge and embrace it. I am reminded of a rather eccentric and devout Anglican whom I knew in my teenage years. A doting cat-lover, he had a shrine to Bast in his rambling house and prayed to her whenever concerned about a missing or unwell feline, seeing no contradiction between this and his devotions to Christ and the saints. The land of the pharaohs makes its presence known throughout the world and across the gulf of time and the supposed barriers of faith.

There is some degree of what polytheists tend to refer to as Unsubstantiated Personal Gnosis (UPG) in this book, but it is flagged up as such where it appears. For readers unfamiliar with this concept, it is direct experience of a deity, other type of entity, or spiritual practice which can add flavour to what might otherwise be dry repetitions of historical or archaeological fact and conjecture. The nature of UPG is such that it is always being added to, and the way a person experiences a deity today may not be how they understand them in a decade's time.

With such a vast period of history it would take a dozen volumes to cover everything of interest – inevitably much has been left out. Perhaps some future book can explore mythical tales in greater depth, look at herbalism, recipes for sacred wines and beers, divination techniques, and many other subjects.

Chapter One

Ancient Egyptian History

In dividing Egyptian history from mythology, we are perpetuating a rather modern conception that these are two quite distinct categories – actual events in the real world and imagined events in a symbolic world. The further back in human history we go, and with Egypt that is a remarkably long stretch, the more closely intertwined these two strands become. However, for the sake of convention let us first consider those events mostly involving mortals and later move on to those involving immortal beings. In laying out the history of Egypt it would be easy to become lost in the convoluted corridors of over five thousand years' worth of events. The intention is to avoid bogging the reader down with an excess of political turmoil, artistic innovations, and scientific discoveries but rather to give sufficient background to the changing cultural milieu to help place the mythology in a wider context.

The geographical region we now know as Egypt was once referred to by its native inhabitants as Kemet, which means the Black Land. Some advocates of African spirituality, such as Molefi Asante (2015), see this as an early reference to the colour of its populations' skin. Whilst there were certainly a lot of black Africans living in that land, the same is true of every other country in Africa which mostly take their names from all sorts of things other than the skin tone of their populations. In the ancient world skin colour was not considered an issue or the bedrock of identity in the way it is in the West these days. Western (predominantly white) historians tend to opt for the explanation that the blackness refers to the colour of the fertile soil deposits left in the aftermath of the Nile inundation. The Egyptians themselves may have had an entirely different explanation from either of the modern ones.

The mythos tells that the chief goddess Aset (called Isis by the Romans and Greeks) was left widowed by her own murderous brother. When declaring her intention to find her husband's corpse, the other deities sent her seven magical scorpions to accompany and assist her. Archaeologists unearthing early Egyptian history found evidence for two monarchs whose actual names are unknown, but who are referred to as King Scorpion I and II respectively due to the hieroglyph of an arachnid on their seals. Scorpion II (who may have been King Nar-Mer or possibly Menes) may well be the man responsible for uniting upper and lower kingdoms of Egypt. Was he one of the magical scorpions that served the will of the wandering goddess? Maybe, or perhaps that is just too whimsical for words!

The unification of the two kingdoms under the first dynasty of pharaohs took place somewhere around 3100BCE, which is also approximately the same period in which the hieroglyphic script began to develop. This pictographic means of communication comes under the aegis of the ibis-headed deity Tehuti and his consort Seshet, goddess of the library. That a religion should recognise the sanctity of libraries and reverence a guardian spirit of them is a thing of wonder in itself. What must she make of the contempt for libraries expressed by recent waves of British politicians, who regard the funding of such resources as a necessary loss during times of so-called austerity? Speaking of lost glories, the marvel that was the Library of Alexandria could trace its roots back to the Egyptian devotion to Seshet and her collection of papyri. Tutelary spirit of architecture, mathematics, astronomy and literacy, she is also the divine precursor to that other famed child of Alexandria, the philosopher and academic Hypatia. A lecturer in the University of the city, her brutal murder in the March of 415CE has been marked as a martyr's day by people seeing her as an icon of feminism, rationalism, and paganism alike.

Geography played a significant role in shaping the spirituality of Kemet. The cycles of the Nile formed the basis of the festival calendar, with a number of deities directly connected to the mighty waters. Hapi is the chief deity of the Nile, an androgynous entity depicted with blue skin, who was the embodiment of the annual inundation of flood waters that usually occurred around late June or early July. Whilst a lot of modern texts refer to Hapi as male, ancient artistic depictions combine both sexual characteristics so this section of the book will utilise the gender-neutral pronouns they and theirs when talking of Hapi or other deities who do not fit into a male-female dyad. This is not done to please Hapi, who has expressed no concern one way or another over issues of pronouns to this author at least. Rather it is in recognition that this pronoun issue has become a highly contentious one in the last few years and that some readers might feel uncomfortable if male gender is imposed on a being that is not, per se, male. That said, it is debatable to what extent any deity is male or female in the same way that a human is perceived to be.

The division of the land into two kingdoms was also reflected in the mythical dimension. The fertile delta of Lower Egypt was under the guardianship of both hawk-headed Heru and the cobra goddess Wadjet. The long stretch of Upper Egypt fell beneath the shadow of the vulture wings of Nekhbet, who ensured that the dark soil forming strips along the river banks remained fertile. The much larger reaches of the blazing desert, itself an Egyptian word derived from the red colour of the parched earth, was the unenviable dominion of the ginger deity Setekh, uncle to Heru.

The land of Kemet was formed of forty-two tribal areas called *sepatu*. There were twenty-two located in Upper Egypt and twenty in the Lower kingdom, each with their own hieroglyphic standard and local deities. For example, the 13th *sepat* of Upper Egypt was Atef-Khent (called Lycopolis by the Greeks) was the protectorate of the wolf-headed Wepwawet. Some people interpret Wepwawet as jackal-headed, but he comes to me as a desert wolf, an issue we will return to in the chapter on deities. This structure echoes into the afterlife, where the soul of the recently deceased arrives in the hall of judgement to stand before the forty-two Assessors who each ask a question concerning the individual's moral behaviour in life. Each of the *sepatu* had a governor, akin to a mayor, called a *heri-tep a'a* some of whom inherited their positions and some of whom were appointed. Democratic election does not appear to be a phenomenon of old Kemet. The 42 Assessors might have been the first governors of each *sepatu*, raised to a new position post-mortem.

Egyptian history is divided into dynastic periods. Manetho, a priest from the third century BCE, recorded the passage of 31 dynasties of pharaohs. These royal families did not rule consecutively but, just to complicate the picture, some ruled different regions of Egypt simultaneously. The first and second dynasties compose the Archaic Period and are charted from the unification of Upper and Lower Egypt, appearing roughly 3200 years before the start of the Common Era, which is marked as the theoretical birth of Jesus. The close of the second dynasty in the year 2686BCE ushers in the start of the Old Kingdom dynasties, consisting of four families reigning in turn until the year 2181BCE. During this period the supreme ruler was referred to as a king rather than a pharaoh, though the practice of viewing the ruler as a living incarnation of deity begun during this time. We know this through priestly records, which act to a large extent as the formal voice of the court. What we don't know is the view of the ordinary Egyptian worker – recording the views of the working classes is an extremely recent practice in the keeping of human history. The king may have wanted to be regarded as a god, but whether all of his citizens saw him as such is a separate and currently unanswerable question.

For many modern people the question of the divinity of kings is purely academic. However, for those 21st century people with a faith in the ancient deities and the teachings preserved by their early scribes, it is one that needs considering. Do deities incarnate in fleshly form or produce children with humans (such as Alexander the Great was commonly believed to be), or is this simply a delusion of egomaniacal tyrants? Without straying too far into another culture, it may be worth contemplating the Roman attitude to this issue. In the Latin-speaking world all humans were regarded as having a divine spark, which for men was referred to as a *genius* and women as a *juno*. This spark for many people may have been quite dim, but the prayers and offerings of others could help fan it to a brighter state. During those phases of Roman history when emperors demanded worship and had temples built to themselves, part of the rationale was that vast numbers of people engaging in the legally required acts of worship would swell the *genius* of the emperor and thus aid his spirit in guiding his mortal mind to sagacious and judicious acts that would strengthen the empire. Given what we now know of some god-emperors, it is hard to credit that all this worship did much more than swell already gargantuan and delusional egos into taking ever more unhinged actions. Exactly the same could be seen throughout the 20th and into the 21st centuries with our more demented world leaders who clearly want to be worshipped by their populaces. The Egyptians subscribed to the notion of a multi-aspected human entity (an idea further discussed in Chapters Two and Six), some parts of which could benefit from the reverence of the living.

What actually is worship, or *dua* to use the Egyptian term? Worship comes from the Anglo-Saxon word *weorth-scope*, which means to give value or worth to something or someone. The act of giving value can be done in a variety of ways – we can tell other people that we love them, praise them as intelligent or brave or kind; we value objects or services by the amount of money we are prepared to part with to obtain them; we can indicate how much we value a person or a pet simply by the amount of time we want to spend in their company, or how much we value an activity by the duration of time spent engaging in it.

The French sociologist Pierre Bourdieu coined the term habitus, which we will return to later in the book, but in brief it is a set of ingrained habits that not only structures life but also shapes identity. To an extent someone's personality drives the kinds of habits they develop, but those habits in turn start to change and develop the personality. The significance of this idea at this juncture is that *worth-scope* could well be considered a form of habitus. To give a secular example of how the process of giving worth shapes life (and how the end of giving worth can alter life, often for the worse) please imagine an elderly man, Bob Jones, who has an old dog, Patch. Bob loves Patch, dotes on him and has lived with him for fifteen years. This devotion between man and dog shapes Mr Jones' life, gives it pattern or habitus – he walks Patch every morning and evening and hurries home when out shopping to ensure that Patch is not alone for too long; once a fortnight he goes to the pet shop to buy dog food and every Christmas gets Patch a new chew toy; he puts aside money not only for the pet food but for visits to the veterinary clinic. One day Patch dies. Overnight Bob no longer needs to get up early to go walkies and has no evening walks to rush home for either, and gets less exercise as a result. He no longer chats to the fellow dog walkers he used to pass each day nor to the cashier at the pet shop, becoming a little lonelier and more isolated in the process. Bob lives alone and Patch was the only living being he regularly spoke to in the evenings, now most days he is virtually silent. With Patch gone Bob no longer has any physical contact with another living being – stroking his dog, holding his paw and so on were little joys each day in an old man's life which he now no longer has. The lack of tactile presence can be one of the most crippling losses a human can experience. He will, of course, save a fair amount of money now he is no longer buying dog chow, paying vet bills and so forth, but this spare cash may seem scant comfort to him.

That Jones had valued his dog had transformed the shape of his life, just as the departure of Patch has changed it again. If we can accept that one little old dog has such a significant effect on someone's life, how much greater a change comes into a person's life with the birth of a beloved child, or finding the love of their life, or being bowled over by the presence of a Divine being who chooses them? To truly value another being, of whatever sort, is change not only the pattern of our life but also our very sense of self and identity.

In our cynical modern age religious worship has taken on shades of servile bowing and scraping, which it need not possess at all. In which context did ancient peoples worship their kings, emperors, or pharaohs? For some it may have been largely a box ticking exercise that had to be gone through for fear of repercussions if they opted out, for others it may have been a genuine reverence of a living deity, whilst yet others may have adopted a practical approach that anything which might have made a ruler wiser and more generous was worth a try.

A more vital question is how this translates into the 21st century – there are no longer pharaohs in Egypt (though some individuals in other parts of the world lay claim to that title), but should devotees of the old deities make efforts to reverence the spirit of whoever leads the country in which they live? The prospect of having to worship any of the recent Prime Ministers makes this British author mildly nauseous, but maybe by not directly addressing the spirits of the individuals important to us (be that at a personal level, or a governmental one) we are missing a significant aspect of the culture we draw from? We live in a more democratic age in the West and many parts of the East, and this author cannot imagine many people wishing to return to the days of serried ranks bowing their knees before a super-rich few (though undoubtedly many of our current super-rich elite would quite enjoy that, and I shall judiciously avoid any mention of celebrity culture and populist wealthy politicians and media magnates who snap their fingers and have legions bowing before them), however more people might be willing to make offerings for the soul-growth of their various loved ones irrespective of social class.

The first king of the Old Kingdom was Djoser, who had the first step pyramid built at Saqqara. Subsequent rulers of this time went on to build many of the other amazing pyramids, temples, and monuments that stand to this very day. Science, architecture, metallurgy, medicine, and many other complex skills flourished during this period. The end of the Old Kingdom led to the emergence of the First Intermediate Period, though there is some historical ambiguity over whether there were four dynasties during this period or they are better understood as an overspill of the previous phase. The Egyptians themselves did not break their own history down into these phases; rather they are an historical structure used by modern academics to more readily arrange confusing episodes of ancient history.

The Middle Kingdom commenced with the eleventh dynasty and lasted for over 140 years; a period marked by an element of internal strife with battles between rival royal families. This period is also known for having the first verifiable female pharaoh, Sobekneferu (there is an earlier contender for this role, but she may be apocryphal).

When Queen Sobekneferu died in 1802BCE, seemingly without heirs, the Middle Kingdom started to dwindle down and eventually entered the Second Intermediate Period in 1650BCE with the dominance of the Hyksos, a group of uncertain nationality whose influence on Egypt will be discussed shortly. The period ended with the expulsion of the much-resented Hyksos and the restoration of native rulers in the guise of the seventeenth dynasty. We will return to the question of the Hyksos further into the book given that they had a significant impact on theology and mythology.

The New Kingdom was, in effect, a return to the old rule and an advance in the power and status of Egypt. Just as the Middle Kingdom had Sobekneferu, so the New Kingdom had Queen Hatshepsut to demonstrate the level of power that a woman could wield. This era also introduced a new force to Egyptian religion, maybe even to world religion although that's open to contention, in the form of Akhenaten's introduction of monotheism. A deeply divisive character, he came to the throne under the name of Amenhotep IV but declared a spiritual conversion which led him to see the Aten sun disc as the one and only deity. In a move that foreshadowed the world to come, his devotion was so intense that he wished to impose it on everyone else. During his reign in the mid-1300sBCE Akhenaten closed down the other temples and broke up the priesthoods. This can be seen as at least partly a political move to countermand an overly powerful theocratic hierarchy, as well as an act of religious zeal. After seventeen years on the throne, Akhenaten went to whatever the afterlife had in store for him and the Aten cult rapidly began to wane in popularity as the old ways quickly re-established. By 1332BCE Tutankhamun, a minor figure in the grand list of rulers, had dropped the Aten-element of his initial name and embraced the old gods by adopting the Amun-element. The choice of Amun may have been a conscious decision to reverse the change which the young pharaoh's father had made to his own title, and the affront given to both deities and their potent clergy in the process.

This rather illustrious dynasty went on to produce Rameses the Great and a later Rameses III, both of whom tackled periods of warfare and expansion. By the end of the twentieth dynasty the glories of the previous generations had drastically dwindled largely as a result of endless squabbling amongst the descendants of Rameses III. Power eventually began to shift away from ineffective royals and increasingly into the priesthood of Amun. However, it's worth bearing in mind that those High Priests and Priestesses of the various major cults were often related to the governing royal families anyway, so power was still largely in the hands of the same bloodline. A new family, originally from what is now Libya, took the court for the twenty-second dynasty, in roundabout 945BCE, and stabilised the political scene for the Third Intermediate Period. During the twenty-third dynasty Maatkare, daughter of the Pharaoh Pinedjem I, was given the title of God's Wife of Amun. This religious position became increasingly influential over time, absorbing a number of functions more traditionally associated with the pharaohs.

The stability of the early part of this Period was not destined to last forever, and by the end Persia was on the rise and looking at Egypt with hungry eyes. The Pharaoh Psamtik III lost the battle at Pelusium and eventually his own life when, having been taken prisoner, he was executed by the Persians.

King Cambyses II eventually took the throne of Egypt and ushered in two comparatively brief reigns of Persian influence before Alexander of Macedonia swept them away. The Greek influence will be examined shortly. The Babylonians destroyed the Temple in Jerusalem in 586BCE and, according to biblical sources, many Jews fled to Egypt during the twenty-sixth dynasty. Arguments can be made about the extent of the influence Egyptian culture had over the shaping of early Jewish beliefs, though such theorising is somewhat outside the scope of this book. However, the Egyptian notion of magical words that bring into existence the thing being spoken of does seem remarkably similar to the notion of the Word. The tales of the golem are almost certainly influenced by the stories of shabti, animated clay servants that aid people in the afterlife.

After the death of Alexander in 323BCE, power passed into the hands of his generals, including Ptolemaios who founded the Ptolemy family. The first Ptolemy introduced a new deity, Serapis, to the local pantheon. From a modern, largely secular academic view this deity was a human-generated entity fusing aspects of several Greek and Egyptian gods (such as Apis, Zeus, Asur, and Helios). Whether we should now understand Serapis as some variety of egregore, in the way Chaos Magicians present the concept, or if Ptolemy had a spiritual vision of a new deity no less real than any other, is a matter of philosophical perspective. Hellenic influence spread and a great many Macedonian soldiers settle along the Nile after their retirement from the military. A fair amount on intermarriage integrated the newcomers, though Greek and Egyptian law ran in parallel for different sections of the population. Unfortunately, the Ptolemies were prone to the sort of murderousness that is far from uncommon amongst powerful families, and the infighting became more deadly with each generation that passed. It is not unreasonable to suggest that this society struck a critical period of unrest, in a far cry from the stable days of Rameses the Great, Ptolemy XI (who also bore the title Alexander II) was actually strung up by an irate mob in the year 80BCE after only a few days leading the country. This act of mob justice was at least partly a reaction to his murder of his stepmother and then wife Cleopatra Berenice. Some modern leaders might well benefit from being pursued by irate mobs of citizens. The incestuous nature of many Egyptian royal marriages was well known in the ancient world, and seems utterly grotesque by modern standards. What is not entirely clear from our chronological distance is whether these were weddings in name alone with sexual liaisons taking place discreetly with third parties, or if any subsequent heirs were the actual product of incest. Many royal and aristocratic families the world over have engaged in so much inbreeding over the centuries that the state of world politics becomes sadly too explicable.

When Cleopatra VII, who probably bore little resemblance to Elizabeth Taylor, attained the throne she made an ill-fated alliance with the burgeoning Roman Empire as a way of protecting Egypt from rival forces. After her death (whether or not at the fangs of a snake) in the year 30BCE, the rule of the

Ptolemies ended and Egypt came fully under Roman dominion. The once great empire was now simply a province, Aegyptus.

The Black Land had seen periods of religious changes and innovation with the re-visioning of the Aten cult under Akhenaten and the introduction of Serapis and Greek cultural concepts many centuries later. More changes were to come under Roman rule, firstly with the influx of Jews to the city of Alexandria following the destruction of the Temple in Jerusalem in the year 70CE. Later on, the beautiful youth Antinous drowned in the Nile – an auspicious death by Egyptian standards – and reports were made to his utterly devoted lover, the Emperor Hadrian, of the lad being seen in visions. Soon Antinous was declared a deity and temples to him were built all across the Roman Empire as well as an entire Egyptian city built in his honour, Antinoöpolis. Throughout this period Christianity was also spreading across innumerable countries. Alexandria became the seat for a Patriarch around the year 33CE, when Jesus was only just cold in his grave (or the tomb only just empty, depending on your view of the crucifixion story). The transition to Christianity is often described as a relatively smooth one, without any great conflict with the older religion of the land. Some historians have suggested that there were a number of similarities between the ancient and new religions, sufficient that clever missionaries could play upon them and draw analogies between the dying and resurrecting Asur and Jesus, making the conversion more palatable for the ordinary Egyptian. Others have remarked that the old priesthoods had been undermined so many times by successive waves of invaders that they were too weak to oppose the increasingly militant and politically savvy missionaries.

Whilst Christianity and Judaism were sweeping into the land, so the infrastructure of Rome enabled the outward passage of the goddess whom the Romans called Isis to every corner of the empire, including a temple on the site of what is now St Paul's Cathedral in London.

Queen Zenobia of Palmyra briefly wrested control of the province from the Romans in the late 200sCE, but they gained it back until the collapse of Rome itself in the 5th century. For a while Egypt came under Byzantine rule. Following rapidly on from this an equally zealous form of monotheism swept into the land under the direction of the Caliph Umar in 639CE. Whilst there were tussles back and forth, Egypt has remained an Islamic country to this very day with only small-scale representation from other religions. Whilst the history of Egypt has continued with countless twists and turns since Umar's day, the arrival of Islam largely sealed the tomb on the organised worship of the ancient deities. The Egyptians themselves placed less and less worth on a religion that Islam roundly condemns as *shirk* (polytheism), about the worst thing imaginable in the eyes of the compliers of the Quran. Many old temples were vandalised, innumerable papyri burnt, and European demand for supposed medical cures made from ground up mummies led to much desecration of the dead. Raiding tombs was nothing new, with corrupt pagan priests centuries before this sometimes desecrating the places they were meant to preserve. Not all Muslims condemned their pagan ancestors, eccentric poets and academics often strayed into areas that mainstream Islamic belief might well disparage. There are also some strong magical traditions found in Muslim countries, often drawing on persistent older beliefs combined with the peripheral teachings within the Quran on such matters as the djinn – powerful spirits (many would suggest altered forms of deities of Pagan Arabia) that are neither angels nor devils, but of a whole other order of being.

The issue of the calendar can be almost as confusing as the matter of charting longer periods of time. The Egyptians divided the year into three seasons beginning with Akhet, the time of inundation, followed by the sowing season of Peret, and finishing with the harvest season of Shemu. Each season was four months long, with the list of months given below. In addition to this passage of months there are five additional days, referred to as epagomenal days by historians, which exist outside of time, neither in the old year ending nor the next year beginning. On each of these days the birth of one of the chief deities is celebrated (in order, they are Asur, Heru, Setekh, Aset, and Nebet-het).

MONTHS OF THE EGYPTIAN YEAR

Akhet (flooding season) -	Tekh
	Menkhet
	Het-Heru
	Nehebkau
Peret (sowing season) -	Shefbedet
	Rekehwer
	Rekehnedjes
	Renenutet
Shemu (harvest season) -	Khons
	Khentkhety
	Ipet-hemet
	Wepet-Renpet (or Mesut-Re)

More detail is provided on this calendar in Chapter Seven. The timing of each New Year depended on the flooding of the Nile, which was foreshadowed by the rise of the Dog Star Sirius (called *Sopdet* by the Egyptians). This was not an exact calendrical date, as January 1st is for modern westerners, but varied by as much as several weeks each year. Therefore, months sometimes varied in their length to accommodate the coming of the Great Flood and the start of the next annual cycle. For modern followers of Egyptian religion, this poses several questions for which no absolutely clear-cut answer exists.

The variability of the calendar caused confusion even in the ancient world, and eventually a civil calendar was developed with fixed dates that approximated the usual times for flooding, the rising of Sirius and so forth. Some festival dates are looked at in Chapter Seven, using the timings of this fixed calendar based on the suggestions of von Beckerath (1980). Alternatively, the reader could do as the Egyptians did for one of their calendrical systems, and use the actual rising of Sirius – the point in time when the star is far enough apart from the sun to be seen distinctly in the early morning. This would necessitate a more flexible calendar. The date when this occurs does vary according to where a person is in the world when they look up at the sky. A person in Egypt will see it at a different date from one in Canada or one in Australia.

Ancient Egyptian religion, as already stated several times, was very rooted in its own geography. It was not a religion that sought to spread itself globally through proselytising (though Egyptian merchants and mercenaries did travel abroad, and temples to their deities were sometimes erected in other parts of the world). It is doubtful if anyone in Karnack 4000 years ago gave a thought to the possibility that one day their goddesses would be reverenced on the banks of the Thames or the foothills of the Appalachians. If a worshipper lives in Helsinki, ought they date their calendar from the rising of the Dog Star in Egypt or from its rising in their own land? There are astronomical websites that provide this information should the reader require it. One could argue either way, and ultimately it depends on what the individual feels to be correct for themselves after consultation with their deities. It is not up to anyone else to dictate the one true way on this matter. If the author's opinion is sought, then I think the very core of a pagan religion is that it is one rooted in the local landscape, or skyscape, rather than some romanticised homeland hundreds or thousands of miles away. Learn when the star rises in your own neighbourhood and plan accordingly. There is also much to be said for studying local waterways, and honouring the tidal passages of the nearest river to the place in which you live. That river will not be Hapi, so attempts to fuse the two may be unhelpful. Rather, learn the name of the entity that is the river and honour it afresh. The principle, to some extent, remains the same even if it is heavily adapted.

An element of confusion is introduced to our understanding of the period because the Egyptians formulated a calendar measured not from an identifiable year zero, but rather starting afresh from the reign of each pharaoh – none of whom had the common decency to die on New Year's Eve, thus allowing their successor to start their brand new reign at the start of a brand new year. The inconsiderate nature of these august rulers was such that they would die willy-nilly, and a second pharaoh would often start a whole new chronological cycle part-way through an existing 12-month cycle.

Egyptian culture went through a number of significant changes as a result of the occupations by other cultures which we have already mentioned – Alexander the Great brought the influence of Greece to the bans of the Nile, and the Romans brought their Latin values and practices. More intriguingly they were also dominated by the Hyksos nation, whose exact identity remains a matter of conjecture to this very day. This unknown peoples came from somewhere to the east of Egypt and swept into the land in 1650BCE. They remained in situ until roughly 1550BCE, when their final monarch was driven out. The early Jewish historian Josephus believed (on the basis of very little evidence, it has to be said) that the Hyksos, whose names can be translated as meaning Shepherd Kings, were the ancient Hebrews. It is a highly controversial suggestion on the part of Josephus, because it seems to utterly contradict the standard story of Exodus given within the Tanakh. In that account the Hebrews were kept as slaves of the Egyptians until Moses led them in a prolonged escape across the desert. If, as Josephus suggests, they were actually the Hyksos then, far from being enslaved, they were actually an occupying army.

However, Josephus may simply have been barking up the wrong tree – certainly his interpretation of the meaning of the word Hyksos is now discredited. There are other possibilities as to the identity of these mysterious invaders. The Canaanites had already occupied an area in the Nile Delta, and at least one Hyksos king had a Canaanite name (whilst people these days often give their children names from other cultures simply because they like the sound of them, royal families in ancient times tended to be more conservative in their choice of nomenclature). Canaan was a sprawling kingdom incorporating the modern countries of Lebanon, Syria, Jordan and Israel. Hyksos is a Greek rendition of the Egyptian phrase *heqa khaseshet*, which simply means rulers of foreign lands and was applied with a broad stroke. Those who find Victorian and Edwardian imperialism cringe-inducing should bear in mind that a patronising attitude to "Johnny foreigner" is endemic to pretty much all empires the world over, not the preserve of one country or even one ethnicity. As a result of this broad attitude to foreigners, some historians contend that the people dominant in Egypt during the 15th dynasty may not have come from a single ethnic group, but have been a general conglomeration of people from various nationalities who ascended to political influence through a combination of warfare, trade and marital alliances. Before moving on entirely from Josephus' conjectures, the Egyptian word *'abiru* (also spelled *habiru*) means dirty or dust-covered was a broadly applied terms for vagabonds, manual labourers, slaves, and social outcastes in general. There is some linguistic speculation, much contested, that the word may have influenced Hebrew. Were this connection ever shown to be true, then it would suggest more the traditional view of the Jews as put-upon labourers than as an occupying aristocracy.

Whatever their ethnic origin, the Hyksos were initially devoted to Baal (which translates as the title Lord, rather than being the personal name of the deity), but became increasingly associated with the flame-haired deity of the desert, Setekh. The Hyksos may have initially regarded this as a form of syncretism, much as could be found throughout the Roman Empire, but perhaps eventually came to embrace the Red God in his own right rather than because of any resemblance to Canaanite deities. This association had something of a public relations backlash for the god following the expulsion of the occupying army, and he seems to have been seen in increasingly malevolent terms by the triumphant Egyptians priesthoods who were restoring the traditional ways.

Some element of contention exists over whether the Hyksos conquered Egypt through violence, as traditionally supposed, or if it was a more subtle cultural take-over resulting from largescale emigration. Anxieties around an overwhelming influx of immigrants exerting political dominance through sheer dint of numbers has a direct echo to the current political picture in the west (as well as countries in other parts of the world), and may well permeate the ways in which historians and archaeologists view the distant past. It doesn't necessarily mean that this is not an accurate assessment of how the Hyksos gained prominence though.

The collapse of Hyksos influence supposedly came about in part when their then ruler demanded that a monarch from Upper Egypt, Seqenenre Tao, should put a stop to hippopotamus hunting (then a popular sport in that part of the world). The improbable reason given is that the Hyksos ruler was unable to sleep because of the roaring of the distressed beasts echoing up the Nile. The German Egyptologist Jan Assmann (2002) has conjectured that a more probable reason is that the hippo was held sacred to Setekh. It may be that the deity himself had asked his devotees to intervene to protect his holy animals, or perhaps the Hyksos king felt that the hunting was an affront to his god and took pre-emptive action, or maybe he was simply an early ecologist who couldn't bear to think of his favourite creatures being depleted through hunting. Whatever the reason, Seqenenre Tao refused to ban his people from their blood-sport. This led to a rebellion, which may seem a little odd (though revolution in the streets of Britain might well occur if a government tried to repeat King Edward II's ban on football or, heaven forfend, car-boot sales) but possibly it was just one act of political interference too many. What Seqenenre Tao started his successors Kamose and Ahmose continued and eventually completed.

The Persians gained dominance over Egypt from 525BCE, but their rule was a discordant one marked by several rebellions and they were finally ousted by the man who succeeded in conquering half the known world. Their presence in the Black Land was perhaps too short to have a significant cultural impact. They returned for a final brief presence in the form of the Sassanid Empire, only to be swept aside by the Caliph's Islamic armies. When the Muslim religion expanded into Egypt, where it has remained to this day, it struggled with the waves of belief that had gone before. During the medieval period Islam was a largely tolerant religion, tolerant of Jews, Christians, and so forth. The previously mentioned distrust of polytheism within the Quran has led to sporadic outbreaks of iconoclasm throughout Islamic history. The most recent wave of destruction against pagan sites, visited by the fanatics of Islamic State upon the antiquities of Syria, is justified with reference to the Quran. The majority of 21st century Muslims are mortified by such actions, but as with the unhinged posturing of Westboro Baptist Church there are glassy-eyed believers who home in on the passages of their chosen scripture to sanctify their hatred and fear. Some members of Islamic State have threatened to destroy Egyptian sites too, but it is fairly certain that the government of Egypt knows the economic value of its pyramids, temples and so forth to the tourist trade and will crush any threat to their wealth if it is in their power to do so.

Alexander the Great arrived in full military style in Egypt

in 332BCE, bringing that mighty nation under Hellenic influence. Reportedly the natives welcomed him in as their deliverer, presumably preferring to live under Alexander than the Persians. The impact was not entirely one way, for the Greeks and Macedonians were in their turn influenced by the Egyptians. Alexander himself, following on from a pilgrimage to one of the temples of Amun-Re, declared himself to be a son of Zeus-Ammon. One of the lasting changes was the introduction of the already mentioned Ptolemy dynasty to govern the two kingdoms for the next three hundred years. Undoubtedly the most famous daughter of this line was Cleopatra. One impact of Grecian values was the transformation in Egyptian artistic styles, perhaps most obvious in terms of funerary depictions of the faces of the dead on coffin boards. It would be very Eurocentric to suggest that the impact was entirely Greeks influencing Egyptians. Whilst they did bring their political structures to the Black Land, they took away a tremendous amount in terms of art, sciences, medicine, spiritual practices, cultural concepts etc. The Greeks and Romans between them disseminated a great deal of Egyptian cultural achievements throughout the world.

The Greeks struggled with the Egyptian language, and the names most western readers now know the old deities by are actually the versions given them by the Greeks. One of the difficulties with the Egyptian language is that the written format frequently drops the use of vowels (a trait shared with Hebrew), so that 21st century linguists are not completely sure how many words should be pronounced. Coptic is the only surviving language that has a relationship to the original language of Kemet, and so modern linguists engaging in transliteration will often take inspiration from the way Copts speak. It is not guaranteed that the original language would have used all the same styles of pronunciation, but it is an educated guess and the best option in lieu of a time machine. There is a letter written around 3200 years ago saying that the dialect of northern

Egyptians was incomprehensible to southerners – an amusing example of yet another north-south divide! The Coptic language has varied dialects, three of which emanated from Upper Egypt and another three from Lower. It seems quite possible that the original language of the Black Land also had varied dialects by region or developing over the course of its long history.

A list of the Greek names of the more commonly known Netjeru is given below, with Kemetic versions (as near as they can be reasonably known) alongside them:

Amun	Yamanu
Anubis	Anpu, or Yinepu
Bastet	Bast
Edjo, Buto	Wadjet
Hathor	Het-Heru, or Het-Hert
Horus	Heru, or Hor
Imouthis	Imhotep
Isis	Aset, Iset, or Ast
Mayet	Ma'at
Neith	Nit, or Net
Nephthys	Nebet-het
Osiris	Asur, or Wesir, or Ausar
Serapis	Asur-hapi
Seth	Setekh, or Set, or Sutekh
Suchos	Sobek, or Sebek
Thoth	Tehuti, or Djehuty

Some names, such as Sekhmet or Ptah, remained fairly constant even under Greek and Roman influence. These names are approximations and there may well have been regional variations within differing dialects and these may also have changed over the duration of centuries.

For historians' questions of exactly how the ancients spoke may be of academic interest. For religious devotees, it impacts directly on the concept of *ren* (magical words) which is explored in more depth in the section on mythology. It also has some relevance for poets wanting to use the same metres and styles as were employed in the Black Land. An underpinning aspect of this idea was that the words had to be correctly pronounced for their magical potency to take effect. If a variety of regional accents did indeed exist, the question arises as to which form of pronunciation was the correct one and which were more mundane ways of speech for daily non-magical conversation. Perhaps the temple priests spoke in the equivalent of BBC Received Pronunciation in order to transform the world around them!

The Romans swept away the Ptolemy's and introduced their own style of governance and culture. They were also a key factor in the transportation of Egyptian ideas around Europe. Temples to Isis flowered all over the Roman empire, though some theological disputes arise as to whether the Isis reverenced in all those temples was simply the name given to that goddess whom the Egyptians called Aset, or if Isis developed into an entirely separate being in her own right. That in itself goes to the theological core of polytheism, defining what a deity actually is and how they come into existence. This question will be partially returned to in the section on mythology, when we look at the concept of divine birthdays. The emperors Titus and Vespasian both believed their lives to have been saved by the aid of Isis.

The mysterious reputation of Egypt was considerably enhanced in the eyes of other cultures by the inability of later post-polytheist generations to translate hieroglyphs. Once knowledge of the syllabary was lost along with the old priests and priestesses, it was not recovered until the discovery of the Rosetta Stone in 1799. This monument had the same text written in three different scripts (Greek, hieroglyphic and Demotic) which enabled translators to begin the slow process of understanding the complex pictographic system. As an increasing number of papyri, wall stelae and so forth could be translated, so whole worlds of understanding and insight opened up to the modern world. In the spring of 2016, a raft of previously unknown tombs were discovered by a dig under project director Maria Nilsson, showing that new monuments are still being found – many with new hieroglyphic writings yet to be translated and disseminated to the world. New knowledge about the ancient land is emerging all the time.

The discovery of the basalt Stone by French soldiers set much of European society afire with passion for all things Egyptian. Museums capitalised upon it and the tourist trade began to flourish with the wealthy and their servants exploring the land and acquiring (by various means, and with debatable ethical standards) antiquities to display in their grand homes – quite a few treasures later finding their way to museum collections. The enthusiasm was revived again with Howard Carter's discovery of the tomb of Tutankhamun in 1922, an era when the mass media was still in its infancy. Images of the fabulous wealth of even a minor monarch such as Tutankhamun were beamed all over the world. Along with stories of glorious artworks and mysterious images came lurid tales of the pharaoh's curse, reaching out to strike down the plunderers of the tomb. The curse of the king, with all the accompanying tales of inexplicable deaths and disasters visiting the archaeological team, seem to have been almost entirely the inventions of journalists – a three act tragedy whipped up out of the death of Lord Carnarvon, the financial backer, and a lot of wishful thinking. Several tombs did carry dire warnings about what would happen to people robbing or otherwise violating their sanctity, but no reliable evidence remains suggesting that these curses ever worked. Though, possibly, if they did work there would be no tomb robbers left alive to report the fact! The infant art of cinematography fell in love and spawned countless films, TV shows and radio broadcasts inspired by Ancient Egypt. The iconic image of the shambling mummy avenging the violation of the tomb is an invention of Hollywood. In 1932 scriptwriter John Balderstone effectively invented a whole new monster, brought memorably to life by British actor Boris Karloff as he lumbered across the silver screen in the tattered rags of 'The Mummy'. We could have a Jungian twinge and suggest that the avenging creature is a manifestation of western guilt at their plundering of the ancient dead of foreign lands, though this author suspects that would be reading far too much into a very simplistic romp.

Whilst for many people the mania for things Egyptian may have been inspired by artistic sensibilities and the air of exotic romance, for others the draw was more mystical and spiritual. A number of esoteric lodges drew inspiration from Egyptian magic and sought contact with the deities and other spirits. Aleister Crowley was but one example of someone who developed complex systems of mysticism based upon teachings from Ancient Egypt. In 1829 the African-American writer David Walker praised Egypt as part of the all-encompassing African spiritual homeland. Edward Wilmot Blyden (1887) likewise saw the marvels of Egypt as part of a transformative narrative that restored Africa as a source of wonder rather than some kind of cultural backwoods from which purportedly civilised western slave owners abducted or garnered their labourers. Cheikh Anta Diop (1988) saw the driving force within Egyptian society as coming from its black populace, rather than any of the other ethnic groups that dwelt there. Diop rather eulogised the gentleness and peacefulness of the black Egyptians, to a degree which may seem a little at odds with the history of warfare and militant expansionism that went on over the first few thousand years. Molefi Asante essentially suggested that the white Greeks purloined almost all their cultural and scientific advances from the black Egyptians, and became part of a European conspiracy to conceal the true source of culture. It is true that centuries-worth of European prattling about the "dark continent" served to downplay Africa as a source of anything other than perceived barbarism and what was imagined to be an almost child-like tribalism – such narratives helping to justify slavery, political and financial exploitation, and the decimation of native species. However, the movement to idealise Kemet as a source of superlative black culture, sometimes referred to as the Egyptocentric approach, too often attracts thinkers who make bizarrely sweeping generalisations in which anything good must, de facto, stem from black Africa and anything bad can be blamed on dubious white Europeans. Those ethnic groups that are neither black African nor white European are largely ignored in such dichotomous discussions. Such arguments are as ludicrous and ill-founded as the opposing pseudo-intellectual posturing of white supremacists. Both groups seem so wrapped up in glorifying themselves that they often curiously ignore the presence of the Indian subcontinent or East Asia as vast cultural, spiritual, and scientific powerhouses capable of rivalling anything that came out of Europe or Africa.

There are a number of black Kemetic groups around the world (primarily in America), which take a rather monotheist approach to the spirituality of Egypt and, by rather controversial extension, a homogenised pan-African religiosity. There is little evidence that the ancients believed in a single deity (unless we give greater credence to the Akhenaten's revisions than they probably deserve), however it is a belief that gives tremendous strength and inspiration to many. This author is largely a pragmatist when it comes to the truth claims of religious and political movements, being less interested in objective truth and more concerned in whether or not the teachings make their devotees better people and more constructive members of society. To paraphrase the Bible, by their fruits shall you know them!

Such groups were not simply a phenomenon of the Victorian era, but continued throughout the 20th century. As late as 1988

Kemetic Orthodoxy was being founded in America by Tamara Siuda. Alongside such organised groups there have been unknown numbers of people worshipping in solitude, or in tiny groups here and there. The author once knew a very devout High Anglican solicitor who regularly prayed to Bast when his cats were ill or absconding, resolving any theological clashes to the contentment of his own conscience. Likewise, there are Egyptian Muslims who adhere to the teachings of the Quran for most of their lives (which vociferously condemns polytheism), but will seek the aid of Tuaret during pregnancy. Whilst such diversions from strict monotheism are highly unorthodox, they are also surprisingly common and many otherwise conventional devotees of mainstream religions somehow reconcile having a foot in two different worlds. Spiritual amphibians, if you like!

Regardless of whether one finds modern movements inspiring or alienating, Kemet continues to provide spiritual structure and habitus to the lives of many people.

Chapter Two

Egyptian Mythology

From an Ancient Egyptian perspective, the world is infused with the Netjeru, the deities who emanate outward from one of a variety of possible demiurges (or First Causes). Whilst some writers allude to the demiurge of their choice as being akin to the Christian or Islamic conception of God, it is highly debatable if the Egyptians themselves ever perceived that primal being as being in any sense a personal deity with an interest in humanity – or much of anything else. This primordial cosmic force was more akin to an impulse than a consciousness. As with the story of Atum, they are often beings that not so much transcend gender as pre-exist it.

The issue of how the Egyptians saw things is one we need to address before moving on. What is a 21st century devotee of one or more Netjeru doing? Is the aim of any such relationship and more-or-less formalised cultus to recreate not only the ceremony of Ancient Egypt but also the mind set? Is the quest to not only walk like an Egyptian but to think like one too? If it is, then arguably it is a quest doomed to fail. Simply put, we do not live in that world, and we might further debate if there ever was a singular mind set (or singular ritual format) to recreate anyway. Did a *hem-netjer*, an Egyptian priest, from the 7th dynasty view their deities and other spirit beings in the exact same way as a *hem-netjer* from the 18th dynasty? Even within the same dynastic period, would a priestess from Upper Egypt think in quite the same way as one from Lower Egypt? Would a devotee of Heru have quite the same philosophy as a *shem*, a follower, of Tuaret?

Look at any other religion on Earth and a plethora of philosophies, ideals, developing ritual traditions, and so forth can be found. No religion exists like a prehistoric fly preserved forever in amber. Religions are living forces; they adapt and change over time and over geography. The search to recreate an idealised perfect past is scuppered by the simple fact that the past they are searching for never existed. Arguably, it is better to form a relationship with one or more deities in the here and now (the geographic variability of here being as important as the chronological exigencies of now) than to harken for the lost age. Be informed by the past, certainly. Seek to understand how others have related to that Netjer, what sort of rituals have been centred on them and why, what times of year were considered sacred to them – but always using that knowledge as a guide to enhance the present, rather than to seek refuge from it.

Egypt presents us with a number of creation myths, each favoured by a different priesthood as it gained social prominence in one or another region of Kemet. Examples of such stories include the Heliopolitan belief that Atum emerged from the formless sea of Nun, sitting atop a primal mound known as *mer* or *benben*, and masturbated the universe into existence. In the early rendition of this story Amun is a being of both genders, and is sometimes referred to as the Great He-She. Different deities were created by them through different bodily processes – sneezing, spitting etc. There are other variations on this theme where a deity or other force of order emerges from nothingness, a point in the cosmic cycle transliterated as Zep Tepi – the First Occasion.

There are creationists in mainstream religions that take their stories absolutely verbatim and consider any contrary scientific evidence or dissenting views as being the products of minds deluded by demonic forces. The author has yet to encounter a Kemetic who genuinely believed that the universe hatched from a gargantuan goose egg. The tales are rather seen as metaphoric and best understood in a symbolic light. They are mythos rather than logos, more of which shortly.

The notion of the formless sea sits quite well with the current scientific theory, as a more poetic way of describing the vast formlessness that existed prior to the Big Bang. The emergence of the *benben* structure could be taken as representative of the introduction of order, and it has a mathematical appeal that order is symbolised by a pyramid. The Theban myth had an even more metaphysical view of the role of Atum, seeing them as not just a first impulse behind physical reality, but as a sort of base material permeating everything else that has ever existed since that Zep Tepi. Every deity, plant, animal, rock, water droplet, photon, gas molecule etc. that has ever existed is, when viewed from a certain angle, a manifestation of Atum. This rather makes the vile way that some living beings treat each other even more grotesque, given that we would therefore be a single entity ripping itself apart. Philosophically it brings home the notion that a wound to one is a wound to all.

The Theban creation story lends itself to a pantheist understanding of the cosmos, in which all things are part of the divine and the Netjeru are not so much gods in the usual sense of the word, but rather ancient primordial beings with a far greater understanding of the cosmos than more short-lived entities such as humans. Rather than being worshipped as such, a person adopting this approach could simply offer them the immense respect due to any entity with a vastly deeper understanding and capacity to influence the world around us.

In the Theban version Amun is more decidedly male, but has a consort Amunet, though they are perhaps better thought of as two sides of a coin rather than as completely separate beings. The masculinisation continued apace, especially as Amun became identified with other deities such as Re and Min. By the Hellenic period the statuary is undeniably male. We could view this in terms of gender politics, or perhaps consider it as part of a process by which Netjer unfold in different ways.

The tales of ancient Egypt come to us via a number of different sources. One of the most influential stories, that of the

Asur and his brother Setekh, comes to us primarily via the Greek writer Plutarch (though Herodotus and Diodorus Siculus also gave versions). Scraps of this story can be found all the way back to the Old Kingdom Pyramid Texts (originally writings on the walls and other surfaces of the pyramids, where no living person was expected to read them). More references to the story of Asur appear in the Book of Coming Forth by Day and various other papyrus scrolls from later in Egyptian history.

The version which Plutarch gives us (which may have undergone alterations from the earlier version – it cannot be said with any certainty how strictly the Greek writer adhered to Egyptian sources) recounts how Asur was a beloved pharaoh, but one with a penchant for travel. Having made many great innovations to his native culture, he then went off to spread the knowledge to assorted parts of the world – Diodorus Siculus also recounts this tale and talks about the spread of agricultural knowledge. Whilst he was off teaching humanity to grow wheat and barley, his sister-wife Aset governed in his stead. This appears to have gone down well with almost all of the Egyptian subjects, with the notable exception of the pharaoh's own brother Setekh. The red-haired lord of the desert plotted the downfall of his own kin, waiting for his return from the latest voyage. A great celebration was held and a being that Plutarch identifies with the Greek monster Typhon presented the court with an elaborately decorated wooden chest – the first sarcophagus – that would be given to whomsoever it fitted. In a gruesome foreshadowing of Cinderella, everyone at the court climbed into the chest, but the only person for whom it was an exact match was the pharaoh himself. As soon as Asur was inside, the lid was slammed shut and nailed down. Plutarch says this occurred in the middle of November, and became a significant date on the festival calendar. The coffin was dragged to the Nile and slung in, where its inhabitant subsequently drowned. Due to this unfortunate demise drowning in the Nile was afterwards held to be an auspicious means of entering the afterlife. Indeed, the youth Antinous who was so beloved by the Emperor Hadrian became deified at least in part because of his premature death in the waters of the Nile.

It was often held in Victorian analyses of Egyptian mythology that this particular saga was, in part, a euhemerised account of an actual early royal dynasty – that Asur, Aset etc. were fictionalised versions of a murdered pharaoh and his consort. Whilst this is certainly a possibility, it fails to address the metaphysical experiences of countless devotees of the Netjeru both ancient and modern who have communed with entities that are very definitely not long-dead humans. The German philosopher Wilhelm Nestle described two broad domains of knowledge, *logos* and *mythos*. Whilst some of his claims are now a trifle contentious (such as his idea that society evolved from mythos into logos), the general conceptualisation is as popular now as when he advanced it in 1940. His contention was that logos represents the domain of rational, logical, empirical knowledge such as is most commonly seen in the hard sciences. Mythos, by contrast, is subjective, intuitive, emotionally engaging and somewhat nebulous – it can be seen as the sort of truth apprehended through art, literature, or religion where we deal with questions of meaning. A logos exponent might study medicine with a view to discovering which medication acts as the most efficient abortifacient, a mythos-guided person would be more inclined to study the topic with a view to establishing whether abortion was morally desirable and if so under which circumstances, or what constitutes personhood and when in the life cycle from conception onwards this can be detected.

In the 21st century many people approach logos as being the superior form of knowledge and mistakenly assume all topics of study can be engaged with in this manner. In ancient times many cultures made no hard-and-fast distinction between history and mythology. These days we regard history as decidedly logos –

Queen Victoria either came to the throne in 1837 or she did not; the question is open to an objective answer which can be evidenced through historical records etc. King Arthur, by contrast, may never have existed and therefore studies of his life are relegated to literary studies and regarded as fictional. Historicity is not a factor that would have been high on the agenda of many ancient record keepers, who were more interested in whether a story moved the audience than whether it had "really" happened.

No doubt many Egyptians believed that Asur had once walked the world, a being of flesh and blood, before becoming translated into Lord of the Afterlife. Whether he did indeed once park his bottom on the royal throne is a topic that may appeal to some contemporary logos-focused historians, but rather misses the point that mythos conveys a different kind of truth which is not reliant on dates, artefacts, and so forth. The people of the Two Kingdoms believed that deceased pharaohs became part of Asur whilst the living pharaohs were manifestations of falcon-headed Heru. For the modern Kemetic this raises an interesting philosophical question – do the Netjeru take ongoing physical manifestation? By ongoing I mean do they live a full human (or other) life, rather than briefly manifest in order to achieve a purpose (as with Hellenic accounts of Zeus sporadically disguising himself as a wandering mortal to test the hospitality of his worshippers). A long-term incarnation lends itself to a notion somewhat akin to the 'American Gods' novel by Neil Gaiman, the idea has potential as much comical as metaphysical. Diodorus describes in his 'Library of History' how the Egyptians likewise believed that the deities, *"visit all the inhabited world, revealing themselves to men in the form of sacred animals, and at times even appearing in the guise of men or in other shapes"*.

The accounts do not speak of children destined to wear the double crown being obvious manifestations of deity, which may suggest that it was not so much a case of a Netjer spending a full life as a mortal but rather that some people became bonded with a divine being once they assumed a position of leadership. Clearly not all pharaohs in the long history of Egypt were particularly wise or benevolent people whose lives were exemplars of what it must be like to be in direct communion with a deity – though it might be conjectures that communing with certain deities might well cause severe instability. So, we may either consider that the fusion was something that didn't always occur, or that perhaps that it was more an occasional visitation by the deity rather than a 24-7 relationship. Diodorus' reference to *"in other shapes"* alludes to the possibility of deities taking forms neither human nor any other kind of animal – perhaps trees (such as the one in which Asur's coffin becomes imbedded when it washes ashore), rocks, or any one of a hundred other possibilities.

Historical speculations aside, a more pressing question may be whether this still happens in the present day. Are there people walking around who have become, for whatever reason, fused with one of the Netjer? Lots of cultures embrace the concept of spirit possession, so it requires no massive stretch of the imagination to think that many people have periods when a vast entity of the kind described in Egyptian sources merges with their consciousness. However, the prospect of people experiencing long term occupation by such a being poses lots of challenging questions about the nature of such a person's daily mental state or how claims of being a living deity might be tested to winnow out the deluded or the malicious (naively assuming that some deities are not themselves capable of being malign).

Whilst the grieving Aset searched for the missing body of her husband, the cunning brother claimed the throne for himself. Assorted travails later, Aset tracked the body to the kingdom of Byblos where it had washed ashore and become entangled in the roots of a sacred tree. The duration of the search is unclear, but must have been a considerable time because the wooden tomb had eventually become absorbed into the trunk of the tree which in turn had been cut down on the orders of the local queen who fancied having it on display in her own palace. Aset disguised herself as a servant, taking care of the queen's infant as part of a plan to gain access to the lost body of her husband. The plan eventually works but, before the corpse can be resurrected, the villainous brother leaps out and hacks the body into fourteen parts (Diodorus says twenty-six parts), scattering them about Egypt. This aspect of the myth resonates with similar tales from other parts of the world, where a deity is dismembered and the places where the parts are strewn become holy locations. When the Hindu goddess Sati died her corpse was carried by a despairing Shiva until the god Vishnu cut it into fifty-two pieces. Where the parts fell to earth, the holy sites of the goddess were created. The 7th century Irish bishop Tírechán relates the story of a pagan holy spring, the waters of which emerge from the grave of an ancient sage (in other words, an old druid) – one of many Irish tales in which bodies of water flow forth from the graves of significant people. It is not too controversial to suggest that Catholicism has absorbed much of this practice, with the burial places of any saints being held sacred, even when the bones have long since been disinterred. Islam equally reveres the burial sites of various major figures, though hard-line Salafists regard this (not without justification) as a hangover from paganism and have sought to destroy some of these sites.

Aset's story does not finish with the mutilation of the body. Not one to give in easily, she tracks down and retrieves thirteen of the segments. The fourteenth part, which most men might regard not only as the most intimate but also the key one, is devoured by the medjed or Oxyrhynchus fish (Mormyrus kannume). The nineteenth *sepat* of Upper Egypt was named after the hungry medjed, and there is a minor deity of the same name alluded to only in a spell within the Book of Coming Forth by Day where he is described as belonging to the house of Asur. This is also one of the *sepatu* where evidence of very early reverencing of the red-haired Netjer Setekh may be found – in the guise of a fish. Thus, the former pharaoh is effectively castrated by his own brother, albeit in a rather cannibalistic manner with incestuous overtones that do not bear thinking about. As a practice this crops up in a number of other cultures too. In 1130 a Welsh prince, Llewelyn, was castrated on the orders of his own great-uncle, Maredudd ap Bleddyn, partially in a move to prevent the younger man from continuing challenging for the throne. Aside from the psychological trauma caused by such an act (not to mention the likelihood of fatal wound infection and massive blood loss), an incomplete male would have lacked political credibility – and the chance of subsequent heirs – in the political atmosphere of the day. If he survived castration Llewelyn was most likely relegated to a celibate order within the Church. Similar practices were to be found in the rest of Europe at that time as well. The Egyptians made quite an art out of attributing symbolism to body parts.

The Piankhi Stela shows that in some parts of Egypt the consumption of fish was forbidden, *"they were unclean and eaters of fish; which is an abomination"*. People in other areas of Egypt regularly consumed fish. Whether modern devotees of the Netjeru wish to adopt the food taboos prevalent in some parts of Egypt is down to them, perhaps following consultation with those said deities. Plutarch makes the slightly surreal claim that because the people of Hardai (the seventeenth *sepat* of Upper Egypt which the Greeks called Cynopolis – the City of Dogs) ate fish, those of oxyrhynchus-worshipping *sepat* of Per-Medjed retaliated by eating dogs. One hopes that this was a misunderstanding on Plutarch's part and that maliciously devouring the totems of rival tribes was not a common custom – though there is something of an echo to the Irish custom of rival tribes felling sacred trees during raids on their enemies' territory. Such habits might have been a mixture of psychological warfare and the conviction that destroying the holy tree would render their enemies vulnerable by robbing them of their mystical protection. Some 21st century pagans might prefer a rosy-spectacled view which does not allow a culture of supposed tree-reverencing druids to condone or even take part in dendricide, but it is possible they did. Equally we may have to consider that the Ancient Egyptians did some things that modern sensibilities find distressing. Freud would doubtless have a field day with the image of a fish swallowing a cock, but the conclusions to which he might have leapt would not necessarily reflect the ideas once current in Egypt. The more politically-minded might see the story of one brother murdering another as a metaphor for the historical displacement of a dynasty devoted to one deity by that of a dynasty devoted to another (such as the Hyksos following Setekh). The hacking of the body might be taken to represent the division of the spoils between a variety of High Priests, princes, or other potentates. The restoration of the body could be taken as the aftermath of the overthrow of the followers of Setekh and the attempt to put things back the way they were (or as close to it as possible, given that the past can never be exactly recreated). There is an overt association between Setekh and Upper Egypt and his nephew with Lower Egypt, with the eventual resolution of the story being the unification of the Two Kingdoms under one leader. So, whether the events describe a single period in Egyptian history, long before the Hyksos, or is a mash-up of varied historical periods into a broad tale or a single saga of the forging of national identity, is now a matter of conjecture. If the myths do incorporate historical elements into a fantastical narrative, this does not detract from their value as mythos – as conveyors of deeper meaning, and as purveyors of the nature of divine beings. In looking at the Netjeru, consider that we are looking at beings some of whom take an active role in guiding human endeavours.

Aset created an artificial member for her husband and bound the body parts together with linen and magical incantations, so forming the first mummified body. Whilst the magic restored him to a kind of existence and enabled him to sire a child with his artificial genitals, he was fundamentally dead and so became ruler of Duat, land of the dead. One version of this story places the fathering of the child after the first discovery of the body in Byblos, whilst it was still intact. Taking a mythos approach to look for meaning within the story leads us to speculate that the loss of his penis alludes to the loss of identity – as husband, father, ruler, but does not mean his legacy (his child) will not live on after him. The Greek writer Diodorus is one of those suggesting the temples of Asur had phallic posts set up in them, representative of the organ created by Aset. Possibly the story of the greedy fish was a bit of ret-con to explain the number of reverential phalli found in various temples. The division of a body can also symbolise other forms of division – of land into smaller territories, of stretches of time into smaller units, of a vast subject into manageable lessons. Kemeticism includes aspects that constitute a mystery religion, insights only revealed to people accepted into the fold of a given Netjer. Through devotion to Asur you may gain a deeper insight into why his body exists in a number of parts, one of which is no longer the original. Through devotion to Setekh you may learn why he tore his brother into sections to start with – because this is not simply a soap opera of jealousy and power grabbing. Through devotion to Aset you may learn how she restored her husband.

We may also need to consider an issue of chronology here, in that the earliest full version of the dismemberment story currently known to exist dates to Plutarch's *Moralia* written around 100CE. The Egyptians of a thousand years earlier may have had the exact same story, or they may have known a different version with some elements of the tale only appearing with the passage of centuries. This is an issue which modern followers of ancient deities need to factor in – notions of what a distant peoples thought may well conflate ideas and practices which were actually separated by a considerable distance of time (such that some philosophies, concepts, or ritual practices which we now treat as generically Kemetic may never have been concurrent).

Asur is commonly depicted with green skin and is tied to the vegetation that grew in the fields following the inundation. A simple naturalistic interpretation of the myth is that Asur's death and resurrection symbolises the season of harvesting and eventual sowing of the seeds that were necessary to sustain both life and Egypt's vast wealth and accompanying power. Some depictions see him as black-skinned, which can be understood in the two alternate explanations for the name of Kemet – either his skin represents the fertile soil, or it is indicative of his mortal African devotees. Whether the choice of material for his replacement organ has significance is a matter for ongoing contemplation. One account suggests a suitably regal golden phallus (which has possibilities if anyone ever opens a pagan sex shop).

The conflicts within the royal court did not cease with the descent of Asur into the west. Aset raised her son to seek *ma'at*, the restoration of the harmonious order. Whilst modern writers often describe Setekh as evil and see him as a satanic figure, it would be better to think of his war against both his brother and nephew as examples of *isfet* – disorder – rather than evil. The red lord is not himself evil, and indeed stands at the front of the solar boat of Re fighting off the monstrous serpent Apepi who embodies all that is *isfet* and chaotic. However, his actions in this story threaten the appointed orderliness of *ma'at*. Once Heru reached adulthood the war between uncle and nephew became even more public. For eighty years the battle raged, with the deities shape-shifting into assorted guises in the struggle for dominance. This aspect of the story is reminiscent of the interminable battle between two druids who take on endless guises, the final of which was two colossal magical bulls owned by rival Irish chieftains in the epic saga of the Táin Bó Cúailnge.

Eventually the Contendings, as they are known, reach a comical and rather rancid conclusion. Setekh and Heru meet to parlay, drinking heavily into the night. The nephew finally passes out drunk and his scheming uncle (who is not as drunk as he pretends) seizes the opportunity to rape his young relative. This ploy is liable to horrify many modern readers, who would understandably regard sexual assault as a monstrous thing reflecting the dishonourable nature of the perpetrator. By the moral standards of Ancient Egypt, the disgrace resides with the victim rather than the rapist. This is an attitude that crops up in a number of early cultures, especially those around the Mediterranean. Pomponius, in discussing Roman law, speaks of men being raped *vi praedonum vel hostium* (by bandits or, if captured, by enemy soldiers) and declares that they should bear no legal shame for this – perhaps suggestive that in the eyes of everyday folk they frequently did to the point where lawmakers felt the need to extend a protective aegis. A number of the 21st century wars raging in Africa see male rape being used as a form of torture. It is not illegal to be raped in the Congo, or other war-torn countries, but the culture is steeped in homophobia and few men would admit to being raped for fear of being thought gay and condemned accordingly. Greek, Roman and Egyptian armies alike would not infrequently abduct, sexually abuse, and prostitute conquered peoples – women, children, and men alike. Those subjected to this sort of horrendous treatment were often enslaved in the process, and so denied the right to refuse the sexual advances of their new owners, or whomever the owners pimped them out to. If the temples of the day objected to this kind of behaviour, it has to be said that very little record of any such objections survives. We may have to accept that some things which we find utterly horrifying today may not have been causes of much concern to the religious devotees of centuries past.

As noted with the Congo, sexual violence against male

prisoners of war is not a phenomenon exclusively of the distant past, but is documented as being quite extensive in many contemporary conflicts too (and widely regarded by researchers such as Mervyn Christian, 2011, as heavily under-reported due to the shame experienced by victims). Whilst less documented than the abysmal levels of sexual violence against women and girls, it is no less damaging to the survivors. As in the past, it is used as a weapon to humiliate and destroy conquered peoples. By violating Heru, Setekh effectively tries to declare him unfit for political office. Luckily for Heru his uncle fails in his intent to penetrate him, whether as a result of drinking too much beer or it being a dark night. Without being too graphic, Setekh succeeds only in frotting the younger Netjer and orgasms between his thighs. Heru flees and eventually tells his mother what has happened. Aset notices that her son is as slovenly in his laundry habits as Monica Lewinsky, and keeps the stained breechcloth for a later plot twist. She advises him to take part in a cunning plot before Setekh has a chance to make his next move of publicly humiliating his late brother's offspring.

Suitably disguised, Heru travels to his uncle's palace and meets an old gardener who accepts the young man's offer of help in tending the vegetable plot. Whilst the old man is off having his elevenses the deity follows his mother's instructions (not a conversation that many families would wish to have) and masturbates over a basket of lettuce picked for Setekh's dinner table. He then slips away. The tossed salad is served up to the master of the palace, who gobbles it down. Lettuce is one of the sacred plants of the Red Lord and was regarded as a male aphrodisiac in Kemet. The notion that certain plants are created by deities, or at least particularly linked to them, is widespread. What this actually means in practice requires some reflection. It may simply be considered that deities, like humans, often have favourite flowers, foods, gems, and whatnot. It may be that some entities, again much like humans with their predilection for selectively breeding everything from rose bushes to race horses, like to fiddle with the genetic development of some species of plant or animal for reasons best known to themselves. Or it might be envisioned that Netjer and similar beings exist at many levels, including physical manifestations in plants, animals, rocks etc.

Oblivious to all the antics in the garden, Setekh made his next move and brought charges against Heru in the court before all the Netjeru that he had been violated and therefore rendered weak and unfit to rule. Modern audiences might wish to simply dismiss this part of the tale as an example of patriarchal values, which for some pagans is about the worst thing it is possible to have. Others might try to translate it into an equivalent modern-day scenario, or seek a hidden symbolism in the events. Heru and his mother refute the charge and demand evidence from CSI Egypt, unintentionally demonstrating that the Netjeru are not omniscient. To prove his claim Setekh engages in the magical craft of *heka*, a form of spoken or sung magic. He intones the *ren*, or sacred name, of his own semen – fully expecting the awakened semen to respond to him from his own nephew's nether regions. Instead the answering voice calls out from where Aset has discreetly deposited the dirty loincloth. Much mirth ensues from the court. Heru not only refutes the charge, but adds one of his own – that he is the one who ill-used Setekh. The same test is insisted upon, and of course Heru's semen answers from the storm god's digestive tract, where it clings to some half-chewed lettuce. Setekh is mortified, as well he might be. What is unclear from the story is whether the *ren* of the semen is the same as that of the whole being – so presumably any toe nail clippings, stray hairs, dropped feathers or other shed body parts might all sing out if the name is called – or if each body part has its own individual name. The latter option could become really quite confusing, and the former option seems the more reasonable possibility. Though given how much dead skin, ear wax, and nasal hairs we shed over the course of a lifetime (not to mention ejaculate), practically the whole world could end up singing out if we called our *renu*. One can but hope, for the sake of sanity, that the *ren* in shed body parts has a shelf life after which it falls silent.

The divine court resolves that Setekh cannot possibly sit upon the throne of the Two Kingdoms, but Heru proves that divinities are far more forgiving than any human might be in such circumstances, and holds out an olive branch. He offers his uncle governance of Upper Egypt, essentially a vavasour position on behalf of the nephew who becomes the overarching pharaoh of the united land. Thus, the Contendings end with peace and future prosperity. In a basic reading of the text Setekh loses the throne because the evidence creates the illusion that he has been raped. As already stated, such views may have been common thousands of years ago but are unlikely to be well received by modern followers of the Netjeru. A more palatable interpretation might be that his malicious scheme had been exposed, and he was thus deemed ethically unfit, or that the scales of *ma'at* necessitated that he fall into the malign trap which he had set.

Another tale involving the use of sacred names is that told of how Aset earned the title Weret-Hekau, She Who is Great in Magic. In the beginning the falcon-headed Re hoarded all the knowledge of the *renu* to himself. The goddess Aset desired to partake in his knowledge, and so fashioned a serpent from mud and sang life into it by creating a brand new *ren*. Stories of this nature may possibly be the influence behind the Jewish concept of a golem, a clay entity animated by the sacred word. The snake was poisonous and bit Re as he passed by. Given that Re had not created the creature and so didn't know its *ren*, he had no power to undo the damage it was causing him. Screaming in agony, he begged for help – and who should appear but Aset to offer aid. However, the help was not without a price and she wangled the secrets of the spoken magic from him in exchange for curing the snakebite. The practical implication of this is that the names can be learnt, and for we mere mortals the most important name to discover is our own. Through meditation, communion with the Netjeru, and whatever other techniques may aid us, we must look within to learn the name of our own souls. In saying name, it might be as well to say learn the sound of our soul, for it amounts to the same thing. Weret-Hekau was not only a title of Aset (and some other Netjeretu) but also a goddess in her own right, and curiously often depicted as a cobra. There may have been a myth once in which the manufactured poisonous snake became that deity.

Our *ren* is not Gladys, Dwayne or Maureen (at least one hopes it isn't), but something far more primal in the language of the Gods. This is, one might argue, essentially what *heka* is – the original language of the Netjeru themselves, the very language of the universe. To speak the *ren* is to make the thing exist. That you and I, dear reader, exist suggests that someone once spoke our *ren*. If we learn to speak of ourselves once again, our divine spark – our *ka* – may awaken and transform our consciousness in a way that rarely happens. It would be somewhat impractical, and rather hubristic, to try and learn the *ren* of everything on Earth. It would also assume that human vocal chords are capable of pronouncing all those *renu* correctly. Maybe the secret name of Sobek is something that only a crocodile could correctly enunciate. The Netjeru alone know who or what might be able to say the soul-name of a jellyfish. Are creatures devoid of vocal chords excluded from the chorus of existence, or does the concept of spoken magic somehow embrace those who cannot, in the usual sense of the word, speak?

The *ren* is one part of the living entity and one tradition had it that the snake goddess Renenutet acted as a divine distributor of the *renu* to the new born (though other linguists dispute this interpretation of her title). To discover the true name of your own soul, meditation focused on Renenet is advised. Egyptian texts outline the notion that a living being actually consists of multiple aspects, the precise number varies by text, but is frequently nine. These nine will be returned to in more depth in Chapter Six, but a brief overview will be given here. The *Ab* is the heart, regarded as the seat of emotions, the capacity for joy, and moral conscience. It is this part that is weighed against the feather of truth in the afterlife, to find if the person is good enough to enter the place of rest. Possibly this part may be absent in psychopaths. The *Ba* is the unique character of personality of a living being or object, usually depicted in art as a human-headed bird. The *Ba* lives on after death and can continue to impact the material world. The *Sheut* is the shadow, both in the basic English meaning of the word but also with an unclear implication that it links to jackal-headed Anpu and the forces of death. Without straying too far into Taoist territory, it may be that the spark of death is forever present in the living and vice versa. Or we could consider this akin to Freud's notion of Thanatos, the death-instinct (with *Ab* being the Eros, life-instinct by contrast), though that may be stretching the point a little. In a roasting hot land, shade is a wonderful thing and not something to be fearful of. It could also be regarded as the extent of the influence we each place over the world, the poetic shadow that we cast.

The *Akh* is the intellectual force of the living person which persists after death to become their post-mortem Self, if the correct funeral rites are performed to unite the *Ba* and the *Ka* to become this ongoing presence. It could be sensed by the living as a ghostly presence. The term became synonymous with the *Akhu*, the happy and respected ancestors who are content in the afterlife. Where the rites were not performed, or the mind was a tormented thing whilst alive, the person risked becoming part of the *Mutu* at death, the company of angry and disconsolate ghosts who plague the living. An almost identical concept can be found in Rome, China, Japan, and assorted other cultures. The *Ka* is the spark of life, created by the frog-headed midwifery goddess Heket (or in some version the more humanoid Meskhenet) and bound to the flesh for the duration of life. When the flesh dies, it departs – for humans at least. Some things, such as food items, were considered to retain their *kau*, as this is what the *kau* of humans (and possibly some other creatures) consumed when given in offerings. Our actual flesh and blood was the *Khat*, whose destiny is either to rot away and be consumed by worms, or to be mummified, depending on our social station. In contrast the *Sah* emanates from the physical form and takes on material presence in the afterlife as a perfected body, in some respects sounding rather like the concept of an astral body, though it can also be understood as a perfected resurrection of the mummified corpse (restored to vitality rather than as a lurching horror movie monstrosity). Finally, the *Sekhem* is the sense of raw power present in a living creature or object, combined with their will to use it. As an idea *Sekhem* is somewhat like ki in eastern philosophy or the Force in geekology. The correct use of *heka* could be considered a way to awaken and utilise our own reservoir of *Sekhem*.

The use of *heka* is actively encouraged in some texts and seen as a divine gift. The Instructions for Merikara runs, *"[The Netjer] has made for them heka to be weapons to ward off what may happen"*. In some religions magic is often seen as outside the boundaries of what is permissible, whereas within Kemeticism it is far more arguable a gift of the Netjeru to help humanity cope with the problems that beset them.

The last myth to be explored in this short chapter is that detailing the birth of the Netjeret Sekhmet, which again illustrates the notion of magical power speaking beings into existence. In brief, the narrative runs that Re had created humankind and largely left them to their own devices. Humans, however, had not fared well and had not only sunk into wickedness but were also constantly plaguing Re for aid via prayers, offerings, and the like. Driven to distraction by the noise, Re thundered forth the name Sekhmet and the lion goddess landed fully formed upon the desert sand – a being born out of righteous anger with the explicit task to rid humanity of its evil-doers. This she does with great gusto, devouring the cruel and corrupt wherever she encounters them. Humanity, however, proves to be somewhat moreish and Sekhmet begins to rather loosen the definition of wickedness and kept on consuming those who fiddled their tax returns and illegally parked their camels in disabled bays. The surviving humans once again beseeched the deities for aid, and received the recommendation that a great trench should be dug in the desert and filled with a mixture of beer and red ochre. Countless barrels later, the end result was something looking very like a lake of blood – which is exactly what the lioness took it to be when she arrived. She slurped the trench dry and passed out drunk. Upon awakening she had become the gentle cow-headed goddess Het-Heru, who spreads love throughout the world.

Stories of wicked people being eradicated in some terrible expression of divine wrath crop up all over the world, and are likely to be a combination of memories of assorted natural disasters which have been rationalised as being somebodies fault, and a degree of wish fulfilment on the part of those who have been ill-used by horrible people (who so seldom appear to be held to account). Rather like Kali in Hinduism, Sekhmet is not a being one could describe as cuddly or gentle. As presences within the world they have the capacity to be as terrifying as tsunamis or erupting volcanoes. This is not to say that they are permanently in this heart-quaking state, only that they can fly to it very rapidly.

The first enunciation of Sekhmet was marked as the day of her birth, and pretty much all the deities had birthdays. It's a slightly odd notion, and conjures up images of people trying to fit ten thousand candles on a cake. If an entity came into being, it implies there was a time before it existed (or only existed in potential) and possibly there will be a day when it ceases to exist. The death of deities is a matter for considerable reflection, currently outside the scope of this work. However, it could be that there will be a time when a presence can no longer be accessed by mortals, or exists only as a faded memory rather than as an active force. The birthday of a Netjer can be marked in various ways, one being to give thanks that this complex force exists in the cosmos alongside (and as part of) us. To honour the birth of Sobek in February one could give thanks that crocodiles exist – a suitable gift might be to aid charities which ensure they continue to survive by sustaining their environments. It could also be to give thanks that primal lust exists, that we have a capacity to self-heal (crocodiles have phenomenal autoimmune systems that enable them to recover from most wounds even in a filthy environment), and that the primordial age of giant reptiles once happened. Gratitude is an important trait to develop and one easily lost in a culture based so heavily on relentless greed and the need to have more and more, never long content with what we have (be that material possessions, social status, legal advances, or anything else).

The relationship between deities can be very confusing, and the myths largely describe human attempts to place these beings in contexts that make sense to us, even if they don't adequately account for the true complexities of the situation. This process is a two-way street, and not all myths can be dismissed as human inventions. Some originate in visionary experiences where deities have revealed something of their nature to mortals, using language that we apprehend. For anyone who has taught in a school, or raised a child, the process of seeking intelligible ways to explain something to a person who didn't grasp the initial explanation will be familiar. Are Sekhmet and Het-Heru two aspects of one being, rather like the Jain story of a group of blind men trying to work out what an elephant is and all coming away with quite different understandings dependent on which bit of it they were touching? Or perhaps they are more like sisters, related but not actually a singular force. The same relationships are often categorised in different ways in varied parts of Egypt. So, the cow goddess in one place is seen as the daughter of Re, in another as his wife, and elsewhere as his mother. In straight logos-led history, this would be a cause for rejecting some irreconcilable statements as falsehoods. In mythos-led religion, these are metaphorical ways of describing how two cosmic entities relate to one another, and so no singular version need be an exclusive truth.

The link between a goddess of rage and one of love also has rather obvious psychological implications, given that those to whom we feel the greatest belligerence are often people we have formerly held in great affection. The reverse can also be possible through forgiveness and practicing compassion for whatever factors drove the other person to do something that infuriated or outraged us to start with. Reflecting on the transformation of these deities can help achieve comparable changes within us. That there is a goddess inclined to such destructiveness is also a suitable reminder that neither the world nor a religion that celebrates it is, or need be, all sweetness and light. If we do not draw a line in the sand, then all manner of monstrous and abusive behaviour becomes permissible either towards us or towards those in our care. We have fangs and claws for a reason! That which is perverse and corrupted needs to be stopped, and sometimes encounter groups and hugging just don't work.

The mythos event at the culmination of this story became the basis for an annual festival in Egypt celebrated by drinking copious quantities of red-coloured beer. Attaining a state of drunkenness is considered a sacred act, shifting into an altered state of consciousness. The addition of red berries to some home brew, or even just food dye to commercially produced ale, would be an ideal way of commemorating the saving of humanity from divine wrath – and perhaps an annual reminder of what may happen again if we become too immersed in vile behaviour and barbarity. There is no shortage of people in the modern world who might make good lion snacks. Comparatively little is known of what went on at the numerous annual festivities in ancient Kemet, which can both frustrate the modern devotee but also liberate them to inventiveness on their own part. There are a number of books and internet resources which list the names and approximate dates of the known celebrations, and quite often about all that is known of these events is the name and rough time of year when they were held. Beyond that we are in the realm of supposition. We must also consider that much of ancient religion was public – parades through the streets carrying statues, for example – but that the modern world is seldom conducive to such gatherings. So 21st century followers need to think of ways to adapt a public religion to a mostly private sphere.

Whilst the above story describes Sekhmet as a deadly force, she was also the deity to whom people turned for healing and the removal of plagues, injuries and the like. Her temples doubled as hospitals, and indeed many temples also served secondary purposes – as did the priests and priestesses. The holy places of the goddess Seshet were also libraries and her clergy acted as scribes, historians, mathematicians, and so forth. The central temple of Hapi held a device for measuring flood levels, and their followers acted as potamologists (river specialists). Whilst this may seem slightly odd from a modern perspective, consider that the performance of certain (nowadays classed as secular) activities could, if done with the correct mental focus, be deemed as spiritual acts – ways of communing with beings whose essence is present in that activity. Sowing and growing crops is a way of touching the *ka* of Asur; giving birth is to experience Tuaret; aiding a woman to give birth is to partake of the essence of Heqet. A sacred act is not only one involving candles, chanting, incense and the like, but can be as simple as writing a letter to honour Tehuti or tending a grave to honour Anpu.

To conclude this chapter, the myths are not simply quaint

stories, or garbled histories, or simple-minded attempts to explain natural phenomena. They are vast stores of meaning and insight into the nature of the cosmos, the Netjeru, and our own beings. Read them well!

Chapter Three

Cosmology and Worldview

The account below is my rendering of the Heliopolitan creation myth, accounts of which can be found in sources such as Pyramid texts dating back to the fifth and sixth dynasties, numbered by Egyptologists as 1466 and 600. The numbering system dates back to 19th century researchers such as Gaston Maspero and Jean Leclant, helps historians keep track of wall panels in Old Kingdom pyramids. This is only one of a variety of myths concerning the emergence of the cosmos, but it is one of the more engaging ones from a storyteller's point of view. So far myths have just been summarised, but it may interest readers to have a tale "told" to them. Further myths, Egyptian and others, can be heard told on the author's blog – roundtheherne.blogspot.com

In the beginning was Nun – an endless, formless sea of chaos full of unmanifest potential. There was neither sun nor moon nor stars. Time meant nothing then and so whether the sea roiled for a day, a year, or ten million years is a question without meaning or answer. At some stage, and none can say when, a form emerged from the turmoil. The benben was the first shape, the primal manifestation of order – a perfect shape, harmonious in its proportions, perfect in its mathematical balance. The pyramid arose from the swirling morass and from its pinnacle there glowed the first light in the darkness, the star that is forever Atum.

Still time was without existence or meaning, so for how long Atum sat above the pyramid none can say. Be it a day or a million days, eventually they grew bored and lonely being the only entity. Atum was all things and no things – light and dark, heat and cold, male and female. The waters of Nun were all things in potential; in Atum those things became actualised.

They sought pleasure in intimate ways, relishing both the male and female organs which they possessed. Hot grew Atum's breath, and from this emerged Shu, panting and sighing, the first ecstatic groan of creation. Hot grew Atum's body and sweat rolled down the divine brow, beading along the valley of the sacred spine. Gasping and groaning, spittle rolled down and mixed with the sweat of the divine body. From this moisture there arose Tefnut, who brings relief in the heat and ease in the dryness of the desert.

Released from the body of Atum, Shu and Tefnut conjoined, moisture and breeze entwining one another until they in their turn wished to create children to fill the silence with song. Yet first they wished to know more of the dark world in which they dwelt. Out into the dark oceans of Nun they swam, exploring through touch and sensations unknown to all but the deep dwellers of the ocean. Atum, alone upon the pyramid, grieved for the loss of his children and wished to know where they were. Taking out his eye, he set it to fly about the vastness in search of Shu and Tefnut. As the eye gazed it cast forth light, the first to exist in the formless realms of Nun. So light divided from dark and colour emerged as a potential. Time was still uncreated, so the duration of the search cannot be measured but, when finally it proved successful and the offspring were found, the eye wept.

That there should be space for all life, Shu pushed in one direction and Tefnut in another. That which they pushed up became ethereal Nut, her body arching above all and decorated with ten thousand glittering diamonds. That which they pushed down became solid Qeb, the firm yet yielding Earth that rides beneath the sky and holds all that is made manifest. The ten thousand jewels of Qeb are hidden within his dark folds, reserved for the eyes of those who delve deep.

Lovingly Qeb gazes up at his sister-wife and she weeps with joy to see the love, and her sweet tears pool upon his body in rivers, lakes, and ponds. The love and passion that land and sky felt for each other brought forth more beings to walk upon the world. Asur and Aset came forth followed by Setekh and Neheb-het, who each in their turn began to bring forth others. When, in due course, ibis-headed Tehuti came forth he did so as the manifestation of spoken voice, the authoritative speech that creates the beings it describes and names. Through the power of hekau he sang countless beings into existence, recording them in the books of life that are stored in the great library by his wife Seshet.

The Netjeru created not only additional Netjeru but also mortal beings. When the tears of relief and joy wept by the Eye of Atum at finding his lost children finally landed upon the soil of Qeb after spiralling through space they softened the earth to mud and from this the first humans emerged. At first humanity followed the guidance of the Netjeru, but over time they pulled further and further away from the path laid before them. Each person contained within them the seeds of both ma'at and isfet. Some people feed the force of harmony through offerings of orderly thought and action, whilst others foster mayhem and dissolution with offerings of destruction that tear apart the proper order of things.

When Nut sees the wickedness wrought upon the land that is her brother-husband, she weeps not the sweet tears of ecstasy but the salt-bitter tears that fill the vast voids. So often does she sob in grief that the oceans are deeper and wider than any fresh water lake or river ever can be. Such is the thoughtlessness and iniquity of humanity. Yet enough sweet water flows to enable mortal life to continue.

Other versions of the cosmic creation have the great potter Khnum gradually shaping humanity layer by layer – bones, blood, skin etc. One version has the universe hatching from a goose egg. It is possible that some, maybe many, Ancient Egyptians took their local creation myth as actual reality and found alternate accounts peculiar or confusing. It is as likely that they regarded them more like metaphorical poetry – much as 21st century Anglicans now discuss whether the seven days of creation represent vast epochs of time rather than 24-hour days. People can have a belief in the underlying meaning of a tale without taking every detail as actually true. For those who regard their mythos as metaphorical, the coexistence of assorted regional variations is not a challenge to a singular, exclusive truth but simply another way of conveying similar or related ideas. The views of the average person on religious matters are lost to time, as only the opinions of a tiny number of wealthy, educated individuals were ever recorded. Whatever the case may have been with distant ancestors, modern day adherents almost invariably accept a multiplicity of symbolic meanings rather than get into disputes about whether the Hermopolitian account is the one true story or if the Heliopolitan, Memphite, or Theban one is the true description of how the universe came into being.

One of the prominent features of this story is that there was a period in time before each of the Netjeru existed. Unlike Christian or Muslim understandings of deity, wherein the divine force is without beginning or end, the Netjeru have definite beginnings. Indeed, the festival calendar includes birthdays for many of them. Asur also has an ending, though his murder is not a total ending. Many polytheist mythologies from around the world include accounts of deities who die (such as Baldur in Norse myth, Izanami in Shinto myth, and Tailtiu in Irish myth to name a few). Kemetic myth suggests we live in a world where deity does not pre-exist the physical world, but arises out of it after the point of first creation. How we understand the death of deity is a complex challenge.

As already mentioned, the power of the spoken word forms a central part in the creation myth. One or more deities are described as having mastery of *heka*, the spoken or sung magic that can be used to either call new things into existence by the act of naming them or to influence those that already are in this world. The role of language to shape reality has long been a topic of philosophical reflection. Confucius ends his Analects by stating, "Without knowing the force of words, it is impossible to know men".

We can reflect on this at a number of levels. On various occasions, including a 1989 speech, Vaclav Havel condemned the dehumanising power of some words that are used to alter the way people think about the impact of their own or other people's actions. Corporate managers are encouraged to think in terms of units rather than employees, to label someone as a unit is to reduce their humanity. Some might ask to whether it matters – it is much easier to 'streamline' a business, laying off units, than it is to think about sacking actual people and perhaps putting them at risk of losing their homes, struggling to feed their children and so forth. Turning people into units removes their humanity and makes it a great deal easier to treat them as nothing more than numbers being shuffled about on a graph. Such an attitude and the language that enables it may be encouraged as signs of a successful manager or business entrepreneur, but it takes us straight back to the 1840s when Marley reminded Scrooge that, "Mankind was my business. The common welfare was my business."

In 1965 Vaclav Havel gave a speech (later published) entitled, 'On Evasive Thinking', and noted the magical power of language which was being increasingly recognised, albeit in a secular manner:

> "Notice, for example, how often the words we use these days are more important than what we are talking about. The word – as such – has ceased to be a sign for a category, and has gained a kind of occult power to transform one reality into another."

The observation about categories recognises the semiotic power of language – all words are, by their very nature, symbolic and representative whether of objects or concepts or relationships.

This author, amongst others, would question whether there is any real distinction between objects, concepts, and relationships when it comes to our how minds operate or we engage with language. A tea pot is as much an idea as it is an object, and it exists in relationship to me as both its purchaser and frequent user.

Identity politics had not fully manifested as a social movement in 1965, but this quote from Havel's speech was decidedly prescient of the current fixation which increasingly treats the choice of words as more important than the topics under discussion. The Kemetic priesthood would doubtless have understood the profoundly transformative power of language, what Havel calls its occult power, to shift realities (though they would probably have been bewildered by the banality of its current application in western society).

That the meaning of words can and often do change over time is a given. The concept of *renu*, the sacred names of each thing, rather suggests the existence of a core language which is unchanging, speaking it becoming an act of *Ma'a-kheru*, the True Voice of the *ab* or heart. The sacred language is different from day-to-day languages, its usage restricted to very specific circumstances because misuse of it can have disastrous consequences. The name of a creature or object in French, English, Cantonese etc. can often be fairly random (though sometimes is onomatopoeic) in that there is no especial reason why the sound 'dog' should be applied to one of those four-legged furry creatures that barks. There is nothing inherently canine about the sound 'dog' any more than there is about the sounds inu, jukel, or pes. Implicit in what might be termed the doctrine of *renu* is the idea that, because the name creates the thing being named that there is something essential to the sound that means it could only manifest as that being and no other. In English the sound 'dog' has acquired other meanings over time (such as to describe an ugly person, the act of following someone, or a sexual practice that we'll draw a discreet veil over here) and could acquire any number of new meanings in the future. There is nothing essential about the word that means it can only ever be one thing, yet the *renu* create things and there is a sense in which they could not have created anything else – and if used in an act of *heka*, oral magic, they will only have the power original to them. This point is worth noting, that the *renu* have power independent of the beliefs, ideas, or intentions of the individual utilising them – they act according to their nature, not according to the mind-set of the speaker.

This resonates with the Norse tale, *Egil's Saga Skallagrimssonar*, which told of Egil's encounter with Helga, the exceedingly unwell daughter of Thorfinn. A previous visitor to her sick-bed, an unnamed farmer's son, had attempted to heal her with a runic inscription but she had only gotten worse. Egil finds the inscribed whalebone and destroys it because he realises the well-meaning but ill-informed lad had actually used the wrong runes. Which is to say, the runes acted according to their own nature and were not merely an extension of the magician's intentions as is so often suggested in modern day books about magic (regardless of whether we are talking Heathen, Wiccan, Druidic, or any other type of book about magic). The advice of Egil runs:

No man
should notch a rune ~
not without knowing how
to control it. Carved lines
can muddle meddling men.
I counted ten crude runes
cut in that piece of bone.
They've done damage
to your daughter's
health all this time.

Much of the 20th and 21st century approaches to magic, heavily informed by the writings of psychologists and anthropologists who (for the most part) assumed there cannot really be any such thing as magic, tend to see it more as an exercise in positive thinking in which the key issue is the intense focus of the mind on the outcome. The method by which this outcome is achieved is, at best, irrelevant window dressing – simple theatre that helps the magician to attain the state of focus. The actual runes, words, ritual acts and so forth are only relevant in as much as they serve to maintain (or inconveniently disrupt) intention. The author of 'Egil's Saga Skallagrimssonar' (probably, though not indisputably, Snorri Sturluson) would have adamantly rejected this approach – the runes do what they do, and the carver's intention has little to no impact on this. Only an arrogant fool would take a splash approach to use of the runes for magic. A similar view might well have been heard from a more distant Egyptian priest or priestess when it came to the poorly trained using *heka*. Those who did not really understand what they were intoning, who just relied on their own well-meaning intentions to carry them through, would find themselves in trouble and probably harming others in the process. An uneducated person mucking about in a laboratory, mixing chemicals willy-nilly, cannot expect those substances to obey their good intentions and is more likely to blow themselves up or poison someone off than they are to attain their benevolent goal. To many ancient minds, certain magical forces (be they sacred symbols or holy words, between which there is not a great deal of difference) were to be understood in much the same way.

In the Heliopolitan creation myth (indeed, in all of them) the act of creation is not instantaneous but an ongoing process. New forms are regularly being sung into existence. The myths describe a process in which the Netjeru enounce the words that make mountains, rivers, different plant and animal species appear. We might well reflect that we humans also participate in this unfolding process by bringing new things into existence – houses, boats, laptops etc. For a long time, we have also used our knowledge of breeding, long before we understood concepts of genetics, to combine and alter existing plants and animals into new forms, to use existing chemicals and substances to manufacture new ones. Genetic science now places us in a position where we can amend ourselves and other species to the point where we can produce distinctly new lifeforms.

Clearly most of the people who have engaged in invention or genetic manipulation were not singing or intoning things into existence in the manner of some long-dead Egyptian wizard. Does this mean that either the Kemetic means of creation is simply one of several methods and others work just as well; or that the myths are simply poetic metaphors for the articulation of ideas and that the sacred words are not to be understood as actual spoken sounds; or even the possibility that beings created with *heka* have souls and that those created by other routes do not? This latter option raises interesting reflections around animism, which views all things as having a living soul or essence with its own capacity for thought, emotion, volition etc. It is easy enough (for some of us) to see dogs, wrens, butterflies, oak trees, and so forth as having animating spirits. In a world where virtually every artificial object was handmade, it undoubtedly required only a little more imagination to see the lovingly planed and carved chair or inlaid shield as having a soul of its own. These days, when virtually everything is mass produced in factories by machines, it is more of a challenge to imagine or sense a vital and individual spark within the flat-packed wardrobe, the mobile phone, or the plastic plant pot. If the *ren* is to be understood as a spiritual, soul-like essence, are we now in an era when few objects have that presence – and maybe on the precipice of a time when increasing numbers of living beings will be laboratory engineered and equally as plastic and soulless?

If we view the story of the naming of things as poetic rather than actual, then these various myths could describe a process of apprehension rather than creation. Which is to say, the crocodile as a living, breathing, leathery creature exists independent of any observer. The naming of the crocodile does not create it per se, but rather encapsulates its existence in the consciousness of the viewer. We distinguish it – by sight, sound, smell etc. – as a singular being in its own right, recognising it as distinct from surrounding sights, noises, aromas and so forth. Further, in naming it, we begin the process of categorising it such that our minds learn that there are more crocodiles in the world than the first one we clap eyes upon. We could understand this concept of naming as per Jean Piaget's arguments around the ways in which children construct and revise schemata – mental categories for the objects and creatures they see around them, and over time for complex, internalised experiences too (such as love, fear, desire etc.).

All young children have countless initial moments, such as the very first time they see a cat or a dragonfly, where they have no clue what they are experiencing and require an adult or older child to name it for them. At such ages category errors are common, such as a small child who calls all fluffy animals bunnies because they have yet to work out what distinguishes a hamster from a rabbit. Schemata are curious things, because they often develop to a complex level with only a simple degree of input – few parents would take the time to give complex zoological information about lions but a child will rapidly learn to differentiate them from panthers, cheetahs, tigers, and so forth. Our brains are like sponges when it comes to the acquisition of knowledge and it is, of course, a lifelong process. Adults have many initial moments of their own – first time in a new country, first experience of operating some new form of technology, first time of hearing a certain style of music etc. Until a few years ago, this author had no clue that quokkas even existed. If the reader wants to return to metaphysics, it could be suggested that grasping words is like having a key to the knowledge stored within the collective unconscious of our species, such that information begins to flow without any obvious route.

The majority of words we learn to label creatures, places, experiences etc. are neutral terms. Some labels are emotionally charged ones, in a positive or negative way. This is usually most obvious in regards to the words we learn to describe ourselves and other humans. If, upon our first time of seeing a human of a different skin colour, we are told that the word for that person is a hostile, pejorative one then we learn not simply a sound, but also the hatred, fear, or resentment that goes with it. We may equally learn words that are especially glowing and reverential for use with regards to certain sorts of people.

Atum's emergence from formless, undifferentiated chaos can be understood as the emergence of consciousness from what we imagine (because none of us can actually recall it) to be the chaotic experience of the infant, for whom everything may be a blur of colour, consuming noise, random smells and tactile sensations etc. Gradually the eyes, ears, and other sense organs learn to distinguish one thing from another. We learn form and shape, be that of visual objects, sounds or whatever array of senses it is that we are equipped with can detect. The pyramid of structure emerges without Atum bidding it to do so. Later words develop and become refined as we learn the differences between a crocodile, an alligator, and a caiman. It's possible that babies may label things themselves in gurgles and burbles insensible to all but Time Lords, only later changing to utilise the language taught them by adults. Some people, whether as a result of brain damage or other factors, never acquire the language of their parents or care givers, but possibly think in a language entirely of their own. The debate about how language develops, whether aspects of it are hardwired into the biology of the brain or if it is an entirely fluid socially constructed phenomenon, continues unabated in academic circles. We will not become weighed down in such discussions here, but it is just worth noting that western society is experiencing a trend where many people seem averse to biological arguments, perhaps feeling that biology is some kind of straightjacket restricting their self-expression. This perhaps says more about the paucity of scientific education than it does about the validity of the argument and, the more that is revealed, the more it becomes clear that biology and social construction are not opposite ends of a barge pole, but more akin to passionately entwined lovers.

Atum's use of the sacred language to manifest the world could be seen as less the acquisition of an eternal language of the spheres and more the process of the child learning to name and so internalise to consciousness the mental representation of the world they are experiencing, as well as the internal sensations, emotions and so on that they are distinguishing in whatever their mother tongue happens to be. Freud called this internalised conceptualisation an imago. If we take this largely psycho-social reading of the creation myth (which should perhaps be better termed a revelation myth if we follow this line of thought), then it means that there is no magical language of the Gods whose mere utterance can cause reality to transform and new entities to spring into existence.

A religious and a psycho-social interpretation of the myth are not mutually exclusive. It used to be a common argument in biology, coined by Ernst Haeckel, that ontogeny recapitulates phylogeny (the development of a foetus echoes the development of the whole species over a vast stretch of time). The recapitulation theory, though no longer adhered to in biological science, might be applied in a revised form here – that the ontogeny of individual human consciousness replicates the cosmogony of divine consciousness. As a notion this does lift humanity to a status granted it in biblical texts, which is probably rather higher than our species warrants. At the mortal level we may just be learning a native language with which to describe existence, whilst there is also a sacral language by which the Netjeru manifested the cosmos and correct application of which could still engender radical transformations.

Judaism has centralised a similar concept to its teachings, perhaps absorbed during residence in Egypt. The Word which was spoken in the beginning is the first utterance of the holy language, and equally forms the heart of Christianity with the Logos himself. Whilst gematria, a key form of cabalistic mysticism, is as much about number as it is about word, it again reflects the notion that Hebrew is not simply yet another language in the maelstrom of human tongues, but is a sacred language recognised by Adonai and responded to accordingly when applied through magical means (be that to heal the sick, animate a golem, or any of a thousand other potential wondrous acts). Hebrew was once the day-to-day language of the people, and has perhaps acquired this awe-inspiring status as it has become more and more relegated in its usage. The sacred language referred to by the Egyptians was not the one in daily usage on the streets of Abydos, but rather a lexicon reserved for the initiates of the temples and the Netjeru themselves.

Quite a number of cultures have had the notion of a hieratic language little used outside of holy circles. The use of the Latin Mass is an example of this, back in the day when it was common to hear in a church. Out of all the Catholics sitting on pews listening to priests intoning Latin, very few would have understood more than the odd word or phrase. Its very mysteriousness is what gave it the patina of sanctity. The question of 21st century ritual must also address the matter of language – should Kemetics, or any other shade of pagan, conducted their ceremonies in whatever their native language is, or should they attempt to learn at least some key phrases in whatever parlance would have been used by the ancient practitioners of that tradition? Not everyone has a great gift for learning other languages, and the prospect of being obliged to do so may put many people off – especially if there are no classes in which one can learn Ancient Egyptian, proto-Celtic, Ancient Greek etc. as readily as one might take an evening class in French or Italian. The unexplained usage of an ancient tongue could, potentially, recreate the atmosphere of the Latin Mass in which the elite reverently speak the strange words and the laity sits around looking impressed and wondering if they remembered to pay the phone bill. It's worth remembering, I suggest, that this is the very sort of hierarchical and almost exclusionary atmosphere that probably drove quite a few pagans into leaving churches in the first place.

The other great cosmic forces worth reflecting on, alongside the potent power of *renu*, are the opposing powers of *ma'at* and *isfet*. These forces serve both as aspects of creation and moral bedrocks for humanity (and any other species that might engage in moral decisions). *Ma'at*, as mentioned earlier, is a complex word that does not translate readily into one single English word. In terms of creation it embodies order, harmony, structure – a patterned unfolding of things in a way that is pleasing to behold. The golden ratio has been applied in art, architecture, and various other areas to demonstrate that mathematical proportion has a strong role to play in things that we regard as attractive to the eye. This notion carries over into the ethical dimension to determine the most harmonious way to run a society – bearing in mind that morality is essentially about relationships and how we treat other living beings or permit them to treat us. *Ma'at* is not quite goodness as we understand it in the Judeo-Christian sense, rather it is a sense of rightness, duty, civil harmony. The Victorians would have probably grasped the concept quite readily, given their commitment to doing one's duty.

Looking at the Declaration of Innocence, one version of which may be found in the Papyrus of Ani (recorded around 1250 BCE), gives us a sense of both what was expected in terms of *ma'at* and, by contrast, what constituted *isfet* when the standards were not lived up to. As previously mentioned, the Declaration was the list of behaviours which had to be addressed by the newly dead when they appear the 42 Assessors. Each one of these judicial characters demand to know of the soul if it has done something to affront the code of *ma'at* during life. The dead, unable to lie, had to answer truthfully and have their *ab*, or heart, weighed against the feather of truth. Those whose moral deeds outweighed their bad ones could move on to heavenly realms, the rest were devoured by the monster Amemit. The Instruction of Ptahhotep tells us, "*Ma'at* is good and its worth is lasting. It has not been disturbed since the day of its creator, whereas he who transgresses its ordinances is punished." The truth statements demanded of the dead as recorded by the priest Ani (originally translated by Wallis Budge (1895), but here with the archaic turns of phrase rendered into modern English) are as follows:

1. Hail, Usekh-nemmt, who comes forth from Anu, I have not committed sin.
2. Hail, Hept-khet, who comes forth from Kher-aha, I have not committed robbery with violence.
3. Hail, Fenti, who comes forth from Khemenu, I have not stolen.
4. Hail, Am-khaibit, who comes forth from Qernet, I have not slain men and women.
5. Hail, Neha-her, who comes forth from Rasta, I have not stolen grain.
6. Hail, Rururi, who comes forth from Heaven, I have not purloined offerings.
7. Hail, Arfi-em-khet, who comes forth from Suat, I have not stolen the property of God.
8. Hail, Neba, who comes and goes, I have not uttered lies.
9. Hail, Set-qesu, who comes forth from Hensu, I have not carried away food.
10. Hail, Utu-nesert, who comes forth from Het-ka-Ptah, I

have not uttered curses.

11. Hail, Qerrti, who comes forth from Amentet, I have not committed adultery.
12. Hail, Hraf-haf, who comes forth from thy cavern, I have made none to weep.
13. Hail, Basti, who comes forth from Bast, I have not eaten the *ab* (heart).
14. Hail, Ta-retiu, who comes forth from the night, I have not attacked any man.
15. Hail, Unem-snef, who comes forth from the execution chamber, I am not a man of deceit.
16. Hail, Unem-besek, who comes forth from Mabit, I have not stolen cultivated land.
17. Hail, Neb-Maat, who comes forth from Maati, I have not been an eavesdropper.
18. Hail, Tenemiu, who comes forth from Bast, I have not slandered anyone.
19. Hail, Sertiu, who comes forth from Anu, I have not been angry without just cause.
20. Hail, Tutu, who comes forth from Ati, I have not debauched the wife of any man.
21. Hail, Uamenti, who comes forth from the Khebt chamber, I have not debauched the wives of other men.
22. Hail, Maa-antuf, who comes forth from Per-Menu, I have not polluted myself.
23. Hail, Her-uru, who comes forth from Nehatu, I have terrorised none.
24. Hail, Khemiu, who comes forth from Kaui, I have not transgressed the law.
25. Hail, Shet-kheru, who comes forth from Urit, I have not been angry.
26. Hail, Nekhenu, who comes forth from Heqat, I have not shut my ears to the words of truth.
27. Hail, Kenemti, who comes forth from Kenmet, I have not

blasphemed.

28. Hail, An-hetep-f, who comes forth from Sau, I am not a man of violence.

29. Hail, Sera-kheru, who comes forth from Unaset, I have not been a stirrer up of strife.

30. Hail, Neb-heru, who comes forth from Netchfet, I have not acted with undue haste.

31. Hail, Sekhriu, who comes forth from Uten, I have not pried into other's matters.

32. Hail, Neb-abui, who comes forth from Sauti, I have not multiplied my words in speaking.

33. Hail, Nefer-Tem, who comes forth from Het-ka-Ptah, I have wronged none, I have done no evil.

34. Hail, Tem-Sepu, who comes forth from Tetu, I have not worked witchcraft against the king.

35. Hail, Ari-em-ab-f, who comes forth from Tebu, I have never stopped the flow of water of a neighbour.

36. Hail, Ahi, who comes forth from Nu, I have never raised my voice.

37. Hail, Uatch-rekhit, who comes forth from Sau, I have not cursed God.

38. Hail, Neheb-ka, who comes forth from thy cavern, I have not acted with arrogance.

39. Hail, Neheb-nefert, who comes forth from thy cavern, I have not stolen the bread of the gods.

40. Hail, Tcheser-tep, who comes forth from the shrine, I have not carried away the khenfu cakes from the spirits of the dead.

41. Hail, An-af, who comes forth from Maati, I have not snatched away the bread of the child, nor treated with contempt the god of my city.

42. Hail, Hetch-abhu, who comes forth from Ta-she, I have not slain the cattle belonging to the god.

In the chapter on Ethics we will return to the Declaration in more depth to think about what it means for daily behaviour. There are a number of versions of the Declaration, with some evidence to suggest that they could be adapted to different individuals on the basis of their profession (or possibly for anyone in a given walk of life). For example, the tomb of a soldier does not feature the injunction against killing. Some of the moral strictures seem to apply across all known variants, so we may have here a sense of core and more flexible peripheral morals. What is not yet known is when this set of principles first emerged or how long it took for them to be widely accepted across the two kingdoms. Other versions include that found in the Papyrus of Amenneb and the one in the Ryerson Papyrus.

There is a Frisian story told of how a king summonsed all the lawmakers from client kingdoms and commanded them to produce a central code of law instead of all the local tribal variations. Off they sailed to find a peaceful island on which to hammer it out, only for the god Forsetti to appear to them in the midst of a storm. He guided them to Heligoland and instructed them on the new code, which incorporated the best of the existing codes and ditched the dubious parts of them. This tale presents a particular law code as divinely commanded (which does make it rather hard to argue against, as the more cynical may have noted). Law, of course, is not quite the same as morality although it often informs the sorts of laws that politicians pass. The so far discovered accounts of the Declaration do not go into details about how they were given to humanity. There may once have been some myth involving a Netjer revealing them to a particular person, in a manner reminiscent of Moses and the Commandments (the goddess Ma'at seems a likely candidate for this role). Or their origins might have been lost or, in typical Egyptian fashion, there may have been half a dozen myths each suggesting a different Netjer and different circumstances. Not being a culture much given to mass conversions of unbelievers, it is unclear if the people of ancient times expected all humanity to abide by these moral standards, or if it was simply that those who devoted themselves to the Netjeru should do so (and the foreign nations could be left to sort themselves out). Given the propensity to regards themselves as superior to all they encountered, the latter seems quite likely.

We have already mentioned that European expectations of Mother Earth and Father Sky are inverted in Egypt. This alternative approach to gender roles can be seen in other areas. A vignette from the 'Contendings of Heru and Setekh' depicts Re withdrawing from legal proceedings in something of a sulk that suspends the judicial process. Nothing brings Re out of his foul mood until his daughter Het-Heru flashes her genitals at him. Re falls about laughing, regains his joie de vivre and returns to active duty in his godly role. Putting to one side the unfortunate family situation, which these days would probably lead to social workers swooping in, the scenario is highly reminiscent of the Japanese account of the sun goddess Amaterasu's retreat to a cave following a row with her brother, which only ends when the goddess Amenouzume does a comical striptease which causes uproarious laughter. Likewise echoes to the Greek myth of Demeter are clearly evident. When the goddess of the grain is laid low by deep mourning for the loss of her daughter, the elderly nurse Baubo brings her out of this mental cave by singing bawdy sings and flashing her nether regions in a saucy dance. Baubo is described, and quite a number of clay images depict her, as having a very strange body – no head, as such, but a face on her belly (the name Baubo means belly). This could be taken as an example of fantastic grotesquery or, more mundanely, might be a reference to a comedic costume in which dancers painted faces on their stomachs and pretended to talk through their wobbling bellies – the truffle-shuffle from The Goonies film, for those readers of an age to recall it. Anyone in search of an idea for ritual is advised to immediately rush forth in search of face paint or lipstick.

Baubo can be thought of as a *daimon*, and embodiment of the belly-laugh which can lift the weight of grief or emotional burden. The exposure of genitals as a source of humour (and not just female ones, as any man who has attempted the elephant joke or the windmill will attest) is not confined to cultures that take a censorious approach to nudity. Whilst the Greek and Japanese sources have a withdrawn female drawn forth by lewd displays and merriment, the Egyptian version has a male revived to active life by such means. This is consistent with other examples of Kemetic myth changing the gender patterns more commonly seen in European and other mythologies.

The use of humour in religious rituals crops up in a number of cultures. The Romans saw laughter as a way of invoking Jupiter or Jove – a means of becoming, as the word indicates, jovial. Plutarch's description of the Lupercalia ritual to honour the wolf deities tells us that the two lead priests were expected to laugh after having smeared one another with a combination of sacrificial blood and milk (one suspects it may have been something of a forced laugh, but it had to be done). Laughter is an important force to remember in a ritual or generally religious context. The great semiotician Umberto Eco (1986) wrote 'The Name of the Rose', in which a series of murders are committed to prevent people sharing knowledge of a book by Aristotle which praises humour as a virtue. The murderer does not simply wish to destroy the book, but rather to destroy anyone who is interested in reading such a book. The killer's fear is that, if humour is widely accepted as a virtue (by educated readers who would accept the words of a great philosopher like Aristotle without question) then soon enough the educated, and then the masses, would start to laugh at people in authority, to mock the Church, and ultimately to laugh at God as well. The dread which Eco embodies in his villain is a realistic one – the book was published in 1980, an era in which satire was well established and the powerful and self-important (and religious institutions too) were regularly mocked and derided. It is far from unknown for political tyrants to execute both professional comedians and ordinary members of the public who have the affront to ridicule them. The fear of being mocked is hardly confined to medieval Christianity either, as we can readily see from the murders of French cartoonists whose sense of humour offended some hard-line Muslims.

I have no intention of defending murderous sociopaths, however there is some basis of realism to the worries of both real life and fictional tyrants alike. A delightful story by Ray Bradbury, 'Something Wicked This Way Comes', features a sinister circus that comes to town and causes all sorts of problems. Without overly spoiling the tale for readers yet to discover it, the villain of that piece is defeated by the power of laughter. A key point in that tale is that evil is able to exert itself in at least in part because people are cowed by it, yet it is difficult to fear someone that seems ludicrous or laughable.

For anyone whose power and authority rests on quelling people into timid submission through terror, laughter and mockery pose a serious threat. Laughter, in this context, becomes an act of defiance against moral darkness and tyranny. As with the story of Demeter, Amaterasu, or Re despair, shame, and depression can be despots in their own right – heavy burdens to be thrown off with the aid of a good belly laugh and seeing the ridiculousness of the force that has previously seemed only frightening. The first half of one of Agatha Christie's best stories, 'Appointment with Death', is dominated by a particularly vile mental sadist who has her whole family in thrall. By the final chapter they have come to see her not as a monster, but as a pitiable, frustrated failure. Part of being freed from her abuse, is to cease to be afraid of her and to laugh at her instead.

Religious ceremony can easily become all a bit po-faced and deadly serious. This small snippet from the myth of Re is a worthwhile reminder that laughter can be a form of magic in its own right, that religion is and should be fun.

Chapter Four

Ritual Structure and Calendar

Very little is known of how the ancient priests conducted their day-to-day ceremonies nor the extent of variety within them, such as whether the grand public gatherings were conducted in the same way as the rituals to which only the priests themselves were permitted attendance. This chapter will explore some, but by no means all, of the issues involved and provide some guidance for those wishing to create their own Kemetic ceremonies either for the first time or, if they are experienced *shemsu* (Followers), to help with self-reflection.

A number of the various Orders extant in the 20th and 21st centuries have designed and published their own rituals for use by members, and the reader could avail themselves of one of these texts if they have not already done so. Before going further, a short word about the word's ritual and rite: for the purposes of this book the term ritual will be used to describe a ceremony that is performed on a regular basis (such as weekly, monthly, annually etc.) such that people can repeatedly take part in essentially the same event. Rituals, indeed, are most often collective ones intended for groups to mark the same occasions together. The term rite will be reserved for ceremonies which are normally only expected to take place once in the lifetime of each person and marking some important transition or passage in the individual life. Unless we are remarkably unusual, we will each only go through puberty or menopause once in each incarnation. Some rites could occur more than once of course, such as marriage, but the majority of people who get married hopefully assume this will be their only marriage (it would be a little mercenary to be contemplating a second marriage even as one walks up the aisle with the current spouse!). This said;

polygamy was not uncommon amongst the very wealthy of Ancient Egypt though outlawed in many parts of the world today. The topic of marriage will be returned to briefly later in this chapter.

The issue of ritual structure has a number of aspects to approach – most obviously in terms of how to approach the Netjeru and other beings through ceremony, but also the issue of functionality (what ritual is for), material culture (what to use during ritual), preparation (how to get ready for ritual, including the matter of how to dress for it), and allocation within group ritual (who should do what, if there is more than one person participating). For this chapter we will explore the theoretical issues within ritual first before suggesting some possible ritual formats.

Functionality

It is worth reflecting on the purpose of ritual. There is not one singular purpose, but an interlacing numbers of functions. One of the most prominent roles for ceremony is social; to bring the community together. Indeed, it could be added that the act of coming together for shared activities is part of what makes a disparate bunch of people into a community. There are many sorts of shared activities that have a binding function including sports matches, going to the theatre or cinema, even traipsing en masse to work. All these activities have ritualistic aspects to them, though are seldom thought of as religious rituals.

Religious ceremony is usually focused on one or more deities or other types of metaphysical beings. Religious activities can be partly thought of as bringing together people through the sharing of a story. It is our shared stories that help form us as a community and transcend other barriers that may exist between us. When most communities were religiously homogenous, almost everyone would have shared the same stories and been familiar with the imagery that shaped parades, hymns, pilgrimages, liturgies, and all the other features of bonding people together in shared devotions. These days, pagan communities tend to be much smaller, frequently spread over a large geographic area and linked mainly by the web, and often composed of people who are only partially aware of the corpus of stories and their symbolism.

As well as uniting large (or even small) numbers of people, rites also serve to mark the stages within our individual lives – births, marriages, deaths etc. Celebrating the events in each life helps to reinforce that person's place in the wider community, helps them to grow into the transition in a positive way, assists with the transformation of identity, and brings some additional fun into each life. This latter comment is not meant as a flippant one. Life is hard enough for most people, and it can be so easy to get swamped by the demands of daily life that it can easily end up as drudgery. Rites of passage are a way of reminding us to enjoy life rather than merely endure it. Celebration is important, and here we return to the point made at the end of the last chapter that we need to laugh at the darkness that can surround us (or emerge from within us).

Speaking of the business of daily life, ritual grants a pause to step outside the rush, the need to check the latest social media posting, meeting other people's demands, or piling our demands onto another's shoulders. Ritual is a blessed pause to sit and think about other things, be that the unique themes and meanings of each ceremony or the more general presence of deities and spirits in the cosmos and our relationship to them.

When taking the time to plan a ritual, give thought to what the purpose of the ritual is. The aim may be to celebrate some event that has happened in the world, or to mark a major transition in someone's life. It may be to give thanks for what has already occurred or to seek to instigate a future change whether via divine intercession or the application of the celebrants' own powers.

The purpose of the ritual will help to shape exactly what is done during the ceremony, something which will be reflected on in greater depth when discussing the festivals in the annual calendar.

At a philosophical level the acts of social bonding, the reinforcement of collective identity through shared story, the taking of personal time out to focus and encourage tranquillity of the mind and soul – these are all means of establishing *ma'at*. At base ritual is a central means to bring *ma'at* into human society, into our own individual lives, into the world at large. Promoting *ma'at* and defeating *isfet* are two sides of the same coin, and are two factors that can be consciously reflected upon during even the most simple and gentle of rituals.

Material culture

Ninian Smart (1960), the founder of religious studies as an academic subject, spoke at length about the importance of material culture within the world's religions. Material culture consists of the many objects use in a ceremony. These can be purchased, gifted, or hand made. Their importance resides not just in the moment of the ritual, but in their acquisition or creation, in their storage between rituals (where they are objects that outlast a single use), in the significance these things bring to our lives in those intervening moments where we may handle them for cleaning or something of the sort.

Some religions make a great point of eschewing all material possessions; however, Kemeticism is not one of these faiths. The Egyptians lavished enormous effort on creating items of beauty for use before the Netjeru, and there is no reason their modern-day spiritual heirs should not continue to do so. The question of which items to use in rituals is really a personal choice, but one that needs to factor in the wishes of whichever deities or other beings are to be the focus of ceremony.

Having decided what the ritual is in aid of, the individual or group of celebrants can then begin to think about what objects will be required. This will, in turn, lead to the practical issues of who is bringing what. Some further questions may arise, such as whether some items need to be specially made (and who will do it) or if there are items already in the possession of those taking part and are they happy for them to be brought forth. There may be economic considerations as well, if items (or their constituent parts) need to be purchased. Will the cost fall on one person's shoulders or be divided equally amongst the group – bearing in mind that not everyone is likely to have equivalent incomes.

Another aspect of material culture to reflect on is how we understand those curious objects that now fill the display cases in the Egyptology sections of museums around the world. Some objects are known to have a ceremonial function, whilst others are of unknown use (and we must be conscious of the often-unwise temptation to label anything a bit strange or mysterious as "ritualistic"). It is quite tempting to acquire a whole raft of replica or (for the wealthy) original museum pieces, even when we have little to no idea of what to do with them. It is not just Kemetics that are subject to this "talismania" of filling their homes with mystical things that look beautiful but are wont to gather dust because we do very little other than just admire them from afar.

Preparation

Getting ready for ritual includes ensuring that everyone who was asked to bring something has, indeed, arrived at the chosen venue with it. It is invariably worth having a fall-back plan in case some important item is forgotten or the person bringing it is stuck in traffic for three hours.

Aside from ensuring that all the material goodies are in place, whether in solo ritual or group, it may be decided that there are other issues that must be prepared before people can enter the ceremonial space. Religious cultures that have emerged from very hot parts of the world often place great emphasis on cleanliness and ritualistic washing. This may be a full lustral bath or shower or the presentation of a bowl of water and towel at the gateway to the ritual space so each person can wash their hands (or face, or other body parts) before entering in. The cleanliness is at once a practical consideration to avoid bringing dust, grime, body odour, and so forth into a venue where people are aspiring to keep their minds on something more ethereal than the whiffy feet of the person next to them, and a symbolic gesture. In numerous rituals the world over there is a point where participants seek to leave the cares and woes of the daily world behind them when they go to meet their Gods or ancestors. Washing can help attain this psychic cleanliness.

The matter of clothing needs to be decided upon. Some groups simply wear whatever clothing they would normally wear, within reason (if one of the members works at a slaughter yard or mortuary, turning up in work clothes might not be the most pleasant of experiences for everyone else). Some groups aspire to wear clothing in the style of Ancient Egypt, normally based upon what is known of priestly attire. Herodotus talks of the priests shaving their entire bodies for the period of time spent in service at the temple – there are some modern groups in which full-body or partial shaving is the norm, whilst others opt not to go to quite this extent. Iconography shows bald priests, in keeping with the Greek writer's comments that, "Everywhere else, priests of the gods wear their hair long; in Egypt, they are shaven". He also mentions that the priests (and probably priestesses too) were forbidden from wearing clothing made out of animal skins or by-products whilst on temple duties. Modern practitioners might wish to stick to linen or other plant fibres, or perhaps consider modern synthetic materials. Rosalie David (2002) speculates that this may have been partly a means of avoiding wearing animals sacred to the deity. The *sem*-priests, who specialised in funeral preparations, are often depicted wearing leopard skins.

As well as preparing the bodies of attendees, the temple space itself needs preparing. Some people are fortunate enough to have a room in their home or area in the garden that can be dedicated exclusively to being a ritual space. Others have to make do with clearing an area normally used for something else, and then putting it back again after the ceremony is over. Regardless of whether your temple arrangement is permanent or temporary, the lay out and the method of sanctifying it needs some consideration – such issues as whether the altar should be located in a particular direction and where the entrance should be. As Sir Norman Lockyer noted in the late 1800s, some temples are aligned with astronomical phenomena such as sunrise or the appearance of stars at certain points in the year.

Allocation within group ritual

In any gathering of two or more people for the purposes of ritual the question of division of labour will arise – who will do what? There are all sorts of ways to respond to the question, some of which will be influenced by purely pragmatic considerations and others of which may be more ideologically influenced.

The first stage of decision making is to work out what it is that needs doing. Will there be chanting, use of musical instruments, lighting of candles, carrying about of incense or sacred objects, reading of poems, entering of trance states, sharing of (and therefore preparation of) food etc. Some groups may opt for a free choice in which anyone can do anything they feel like doing, regardless. However, even such a laissez-faire approach needs to factor in some plan for what to do if two or more people both want to do the same thing, or if there is some activity that nobody wants to do.

Other groups may prefer some rationale agreed on in advance for the allocation of tasks. It may, for example, be decided to use what Jordan Peterson (2018) refers to as a hierarchy of competence. Some tasks may require particular skills, and whoever is considered best at that activity carries it out (whether they want to or not!). Other groups may favour a division by gender, for which there is evidence stemming from Kemet. Early Egypt seems to have regarded certain ritual activities as the special province of women, whilst other things were for the men to carry out.

The term for a priestess was *hemet-netjer*, and surviving accounts ascribe certain key functions to them. These activities are not necessarily an exhaustive or exclusive list, but just ones commonly referred to (in other words, priestesses may have had assorted other functions not often mentioned by the surviving and translated texts. Use of the term *hemet-netjer* has been traced back at least as far as Old Kingdom texts and inscriptions. The functions attributed to the priestesses forming the *khener*, a combination of orchestra and choir, playing music and singing for ritual. They also engaged in ceremonial dancing, an important feature of many religions the world over. Some priestesses were also termed *shemet*, chanters, which may well suggest that a variety of musical techniques were employed including chants to induce trance-states alongside songs of a celebratory or austere nature. Some of these songs may have been much like the hymns that can be heard in other religions, perhaps employed on a seasonal basis such as particular songs to mark the flooding of the Nile or the receding of its waters. It is possible that some readers may regard these roles as "mere" entertainment ones and of less status or importance than the roles of orating and conducting ceremonies more commonly associated with men. Such a perception would be to do an injustice to the functions of music, dance, and song. We know that singers and musicians enjoyed considerable status in early medieval Ireland and Wales, and clearly some people earn a vast fortune and devoted followings in a secular context these days. There is no reason to suppose that the *hemet-netjer* of Egypt did not enjoy considerable status both in the temple and in wider society if her voice, dancing, or musical talent was exceptionally noteworthy.

The usual word for a man was *tai*, though the term for a specifically male priest was not *tai-netjer*, but rather *hem-netjer*. This has led some historians and other academics to suggest that *hem* were neither women nor, in the usual sense, men. Faris Malik (1999), amongst others, has forwarded the argument that *hem* may have meant eunuch. The duties of these priests included the making of daily offerings at the temples and the conducting of those ceremonies – in general they seem to have taken on a coordinating role, masters of the ceremonies. Frans Jonckheere (1954) explores the issue of eunuchs in Egypt, for whom no direct word has currently been established. He looks at possible words which might have meant eunuch, such as *tkr* (possibly pronounced *taker*). One of the words considered is *hem*, which is used in a variety of contexts suggestive of a third sex alongside male and female as well as arguably being a shortened form of the word for a woman. Malik raises the possibility that a term may have been in use for a non-breeding male which could have incorporated both those whose genitals had been removed but also men who were fully intact but simply had no sexual interest in women, i.e. men who were either asexual or fully homosexual in their tastes. Malik considers *hem* in this light, doubtless influenced by those cultures around the world in which men with minority sexual preferences acquire spiritual roles in society. The term minority is used here advisedly, because such men are not always gay in the way that word is understood in the modern west. These possible interpretations of the word *hem* are really only vague possibilities, and it seems too big a leap to make any definitive statements about the Egyptians having gay, asexual, celibate, or neutered priesthoods or anything of the sort.

Before moving on to other issues, it is worth contemplating the issue of gender from a 21st century perspective. Gender identity is a regular topic of discussion in the newspapers, and an almost daily issue on social media. If your group does decide to have male and female task distinctions, take time to decide firstly how members will define sex and secondly what role will be created for anyone who joins the group who is neither male nor female. For a great many people biological sex and gender are equated, but there are obviously some people for whom this is not the case. If the group states that activity X can only be carried out by women, does this mean only people who are biologically women or does this mean people who identify as women? If the latter, will the group take this purely as self-definition or will there be some physical point – surgical procedures, hormonal injections, or whatever – that the individual will be expected to have passed beyond before the group is happy for them to engage in those activities? These are issues to discuss with the rest of your group, there being no central authority to dictate to you exactly how you must be organised. Though if you live in a country that allows pagan religious groups to register as legal entities on par with a church or synagogue, then the law of the land may impose some official guidance on such matters.

Some people are born intersex, and others identify themselves as genderqueer or one of the related terms. As mentioned earlier, Frans Jonckheere explored the issue of eunuchs in Ancient Egypt, suggesting that some artistic depictions of people with curiously formed bodies actually showed signs typically resulting from either pre- or post-pubertal castration (such as long legs, pendulous breasts and small skulls in the former case). Castration these days is thankfully very rare, and usually the result of medical procedures stemming from cancer or accident (apparently it can happen where motorcyclists are hurled forward over the handlebars during crashes). Some people who have lost all or part of their genitals may feel themselves to still be very much male, whilst others may feel their gender identity to have changed to something different. Only the individual in question is in a position to say how they feel on this. This is quite a small percentage of the population and a group may never encounter anyone from within this demographic, but it is worth knowing how the group consensus views these matters ahead of time rather than being caught on the hoof. If there is a gender-based role allocation, where do people who do not fit into either gender fit within the group?

Whichever decision is made within the group, there is the potentiality that some people may either not want to join it in the first place or that others will feel they can no longer remain. Of course, this does not apply only towards decisions regarding gender issues and all sorts of philosophical stances will include some and exclude others.

Second-wave feminism tended towards essentialism, the conviction that there is something biologically and socially unique and essential to being a woman that a man can never experience and vice versa. This approach tends to suggest that surgery, medication, and so forth cannot give full access to the essential experience of being a man or a woman. Third-wave feminism, heavily influenced by theorists such as Judith Butler (1990), tends towards constructivism and the notion that gender roles are socially invented and shaped, that gender itself is an identity to which anyone (regardless of their biology) can aspire. Exponents of these two ideologies often clash when it comes to how transgendered people and non-binary people are understood (though worth noting that they often agree on other matters). At some stage there will be fourth-wave feminism and only time will tell what stance its adherents will advocate and how warmly or scathingly they will view the stances of the second- and third-wave advocates. It is an extremely sensitive topic and intense emotions can potentially be generated by people within both the essentialist and constructivist camps.

Evidence regarding Ancient Egyptian ideas around third

sexes is scanty, which may be due to a combination of factors. One straightforward factor may be that they did not feature prominently in society at that period. Another issue may be the way in which modern translators understand the hieroglyphs of old – given that most translators come from cultures where gender has mostly been thought of in a binary, the idea that certain words might signify something outside of that duality may simply not have occurred. Some cultures and historical periods have also been inclined to censoriousness about some issues. So for example, a translator from the Edwardian era or one who is a devout Muslim might be inclined to gloss over a passage that appears to describe people engaging in cross-dressing or same-sex love, and either not include the translation in their journal articles of books, or at least render it into a more acceptable form to their likely readers. We also have to factor in the quantity of texts yet to be translated, which may contain all manner of information currently unavailable to academics and the public alike.

In Egyptian society wealthy women enjoyed considerable freedom, were able to own property and run businesses, instigate divorce procedures, and bring court cases. Within the temple structures they were able to enjoy considerable status and freedoms which were not always available to women in other parts of the world or periods of history.

Ann Macy Roth (2000) makes a strong argument that Western medical perceptions consider fertility to be almost exclusively a female issue, giving only minimal attention to male infertility. This, she argues, is a view that roots in wider social attitudes rather than originating in medical understanding. In cultures where a woman's primary value has long been her ability to bear healthy children (especially of the gender favoured either by society or within her family unit), the inability to have any children – or at least socially desirable sorts of children – becomes a stumbling block to her development of social worth. Henry

VIII was notorious for putting aside wives who failed to deliver the healthy male heir that both he and the wider state craved.

She argues that the Ancient Egyptians, by contrast, viewed creativity and fertility as primarily a male function and that this, in part, helped liberate women to achieve status through routes not connected to the number of offspring they could produce.

Sample ritual

To date no ancient papyrus has been unearthed giving clear instructions on how to conduct a ceremony in Kemetic style – assuming, of course, that there was one consistent form of ritual used throughout all the *sepatu* for the several thousand years' worth of history. It seems rather more probable that different regions had their own styles which waxed and waned in popularity over the duration of time. Those rituals which are described commonly involve the Pharaoh in some manner, and it cannot be assumed that these were typical or reflective of the sorts of rituals take place in small local temples on a daily basis.

It is also worth speculating on the possible differences between temple rituals and observances taking place in the home, fields etc. Trained priests may not have been required for all ceremonial acts, though given the sheer volume of people who spent at least a short period of their lives serving in the temples, probably a sizeable portion of the population had some notion as to how to perform ritual.

Many religions have a distinction between what the Greeks termed *oikos* and *polis*, the activities of the private and public spheres. Christians saying Grace round the dinner table do not require the presence of a vicar or priest, but it is nonetheless a ritualistic act. Likewise, Jewish families are not obliged to find a rabbi every time they mark the Sabbath meal. The kinds of ceremonial acts performed in churches and synagogues are of a different order to the sorts of daily, weekly etc. activities taking place in the home.

Do the kinds of rituals engaged in by 21st century Kemetics in their own homes constitute high temple ceremonies full of pomp and grandeur, or should they be more equivalent to the humble activities of the householder of several thousand years ago? Grand operatic ceremonials are highly enjoyable, but do seem better suited to large scale gatherings – perhaps the sort of numbers that might normally only be found during a large annual conference.

Early Egyptian concepts of ritual, philosophy, magic, medicine and so forth were hugely influential in Greece and helped shape how they did things. As Greek culture came to prominence and their military might increased, so the Egyptian began to dwindle. Following the Hellenic occupation of Egypt, the process of influence changed direction, and many Egyptians changed their thinking and practices in response to what were by then independently Hellenic notions. This book is not arguing in favour of a reconstructionist stance, largely because it seems more romantic than practical, but it is worth briefly thinking about this issue with respect to ritual. For those aspiring to engage in rituals that have a degree of authentic connection to the ceremonies of the distant past, the question must be addressed as to which historical period will be recreated. The rituals of early Egypt were somewhat different to the Hellenised ones of the Ptolemaic period. The ideological purist might aspire to a wholly Egyptian style of ceremony uninfluenced by Greeks (and presumably the Hyksos, the Persians, the Romans, and the various other occupying presences). The slightly more pragmatic might opt to have Old Kingdom rituals for the singularly Egyptian deities whilst being open to some Ptolemaic ceremonies for deities identifiably from that era, such as Serapis. Those who regard themselves as Hearers of the Netjeru may be content with devising modern rituals, informed by the past but not strictly circumscribed by it, and await the response of the

Eternals – if they dislike the ritual format, change it, if they are happy with it, all well and good. For what it is worth, this author sits in the latter camp.

The format below is suitable for simple rituals for solitary or small group practice, something that may echo the householder honourings and offerings rather than the grand temple ceremonies. Some pagan traditions, such as Wicca, have commonly used formats for sanctifying space and containing the presences raised or communicated with. There is no indication that the ancients cast a Circle or anything of that sort. Where a ritual occurred in a temple it seems unlikely that the space would be consecrated (much less deconsecrated) each time – rather there would be an important blessing ceremony for the inauguration of the building that would serve for all time. Ceremonies held in temporary locations, such as the blessing of fields, might have involved the conjuring of protections for those involved, even if simply through the use of incense or sprinkling water.

The French archaeologist Alexandre Moret published an account in 1902 of a ritual used for making daily offerings, which he developed from a set of papyrus manuscripts from Karnak about Amun and Mut, written in the first part of the Twenty-second Dynasty. Whilst there is no especial reason to suppose this format was widely used throughout Egypt or over a prolonged period of time, it is certainly a workable format and is presented below as a basic style of ritual.

A Basic Ritual Format

Before starting the ritual, it would be useful to have the following objects present either upon the altar or side table:

Bowl
Jug of fresh water
Candle and matches or a lighter
Jar of natron (see detail below)

Jar of granular incense and charcoal rings and burner (or joss
  sticks)
Kar (a chest, cupboard or other box containing a sacred statue
  or picture)
Wax seal and cords to close the *kar* (or perhaps just a key)
Green and black kohl (eyeliner would do the same job)
Bottle of scented oil
Any additional offerings that are to be made

Real natron, which the Egyptians used in funeral and other rites,
is difficult to lay hands to these days. An approximation can be
made by mixing equal quantities of salt and baking powder.
Quite a few Kemetics like to enhance this recipe by mixing in a
little water to create a paste which can then be spread on a baking
tray and left in the oven on the lowest heat for a couple of hours.
Once the mix is dried, but not yet burnt, it can be removed and
left to cool before being broken up and stored somewhere away
from damp atmospheres. Some people also like to use bath salts
as a natron substitute.

As each person enters the shrine, be that an indoor or outdoor
location, the Leader of the ritual (who need not necessarily be
the leader of the whole group but is perhaps the host who has
prepared the venue) bids to each person:

"ii wy em hotep (welcome in peace)"

To which each person should reply:

"Udjer her tenu (greetings to you)"

Each person should move to the allocated place, each in a
position where they can see the *kar* (which the Greeks referred to
as a naos), the chest or cupboard that contains the sacred image.
Each person should already be dressed in whatever the agreed

manner is, and it should go without saying that all mobile phones and other such devices should be turned off or left out of ear-shot. Having said this should not need saying, this author has attended rituals where participants' phones have started ringing, and they've answered them mid-ceremony!

Sit meditating upon the name of the Netjer or other entity that you intend to contact; participants may wish to chant the name aloud or quietly to themselves as agreed upon in advance. If in group ritual, have an agreed upon gesture that each person makes to signify that they have attained a state of mind where they feel ready. Something as simple as raising a hand or placing the palm over the heart is sufficient. In terms of ritual gestures, the act of devotion was known as *dua* and often accompanied by a gesture, the *henu*. This was done by holding both hands out at a 90° angle from the body with the palms turned up to the sky. When your mind is suitably focused, sprinkle incense on some charcoal (or light joss sticks, as preferred). The Leader should say:

"iu wabu di seneter (we offer pure things, giving incense)"

The Netjer or other being that is to be honoured should be represented by a statue, icon, or other focal point. This representation needs to be kept somewhere private when not the focus of ritual. Moret and others have described the inner shrines where the holiest of statues, inhabited by the spirit of the Netjer, was kept away from idle curiosity. Moret details the morning ritual, which involves the unsealing of the shrine doors. These doors had been shut and protected with a seal of wax and rope the evening before. If the temple space is a temporary one that will be returned to a more mundane use after the ceremony, then a practical suggestion is to keep the statue or icon in a portable cupboard or box that can be set up ready. Present the incense before the box, cupboard, or other container. Then break the seal and untie the cord around the door-knobs. You might wish to create or acquire a mould in which hot wax can be poured each night to create a new seal. If this is impractical, then whatever method is used to close the door or lid (such as a key) can be symbolically removed to reveal the statue or icon within.

The Leader bows in front of the Netjer, then kneels down and kisses the ground. He or she raises both arms while singing a hymn. For group ritual each person should join in with either raising their hands or making the *henu* gesture described earlier, and singing. Should your singing voice resemble a cat falling down a mine shaft, it might be better to simply recite the hymn as a poem. A number of possible hymns are included in the chapter on the Netjeru, but as an example of one from a 13th Dynasty papyrus (currently in the British Museum) is included below, the translation having been made by R B Parkinson:

Hail to Sobek of Shedet!
Open be the face of Rahes the gracious,
Heru who is in the midst of Shedet!
O appear Heru upon the rivers!
Rise high, Sobek who is in Shedet,
Re-Heru, mighty god!
Hail to you Sobek of Shedet!
Hail to you, who rise from the Flood,
Heru chief of the Two Lands, bull of bulls, great male, lord of the
island-lands!
Qeb has provided you with your sight, he has united you with your
eyes.
Strong one, your strength is great!
May you go through the Lake-land,
Traverse the Great-Green, and seek out your father Asur.
Now you have found him, and made him live, and said:
This cleans the mouth of his father in his name of Sokar!
You have commanded your children to proceed and care for your

father ~
That is, him – in their name of 'Carers of Sokar';
You have pressed upon the mouth of your father Asur;
You have opened his mouth for him.
You are his Beloved Son; you have saved your father Asur;
You have protected.

When the hymn is finished burn more incense, pour some fresh water into a bowl on the altar and add a pinch of natron, then present a bottle of scented oil to the sacred image. The choice of fragrant oil should be relevant to the Netjer, with some suggestions being offered on this matter in the chapter on the Netjeru. The oil can be anointed on the statue or icon if suitable and a little should be dabbed over the third eye or pineal gland of each person presence.

Unless you are honouring the Netjeret Ma'at herself as the central part of the ritual, now is the time to make an offering to the concept of *ma'at* itself. The following short extract from the Instructions of Ptahhotep makes a nice shared call to the Netjeret of order and harmony which the Leader could say and then everyone follows by saying Dua Ma'at. The Leader might wish to hold up an ostrich feather whilst the recitation is made, placing it upon the altar afterwards. If an actual ostrich feather is difficult to locate, symbolic ones made of silver, clay etc. can be purchased or created. You may wish to substitute a different call to Ma'at from an ancient source or of your own devising.

Ma'at is good and its worth is lasting.
It has not been disturbed since the day of its creator,
whereas he who transgresses its ordinances is punished.
It lies as a path in front even of him who knows nothing.
Wrongdoing has never yet brought its venture to port.
It is true that evil may gain wealth but the strength of truth is that it lasts;

a man can say: "It was the property of my father."
Dua Ma'at, dua Ma'at, dua Ma'at!

This makes a suitable point in the ritual to pause and consider ways in which to make life a little more orderly and harmonious during the coming day. Alexandre Moret (1902) described the next stage as being the dressing or draping of the sacred statue with four rolls of material and the decorating of its eyes with green and black cosmetics. This may not be practical, depending on the size of the statue and the type of material it is made from. If it is unworkable, other steps can be taken. As a practical suggestion, clothe the statue in at least one piece of material kept solely for this purpose. If you are using an icon or picture rather than a statue, the material could be laid across the top of the frame. If it is inappropriate to use the kinds of cosmetics described, try two tiny dots of colour on the pupils of the statue – the practice of painting in the pupils of holy statues to bring them to life is found in many cultures around the world. With a picture, these dots could be placed on the glass of the frame if you are worried about damaging the image with regular adding and removing of face paint.

Moret does not note it, but this would be a suitable point in the procedure to call the words of awakening, which is the meaning of the word *nehesi*.

Nehesi Sobek [or name of the relevant Netjer]!
Nehesi em hotep!
Nehesi nefer.
Nehesi, nehesi, nehesi!

At this juncture, each person should have the chance to speak to the deity either aloud or quietly in thought alone. The ritual Moret described is one for the making of morning offerings, which would make it suitable to contemplate the day ahead and any advice or aid required with what is to come. If this style of ritual is not marking the start of the day but occurring at some later point, then it could be used as a form of consultation with the deity in which a problem is presented and then an answer sought via divination, meditation, or some other method.

The offerings Moret refers to are prayers, incense, and the kohl make-up for the eyes. If this is more than a morning greeting to the deity, ancestral presence, or whatever other entity you might wish to speak to, then more substantial offerings might be made following the consultation as a means of expressing gratitude. The chapter on the deities contains suggestions about such offerings. This chapter will also address the question of why a vastly potent spirit-being would want bowls of wine, fruit, and the like.

Each person can make their offering of whatever sort seems appropriate.

As the ceremony draws to its close the Leader wafts the incense in front of the statue and leads the withdrawal from the shrine, normally walking out backwards whilst bowing the head to the sacred statue. If the ceremony takes place outdoors and any footprints have been left in the soil or sand, these should be swept away with a small brush so that the sacred area is without blemish. Some groups engage in the act of 'Removing the Foot' even if they are indoors or on a hard surface. The Leader could say the following with everyone joining in on the last three words:

"pet em hotep, ta em hotep. Ankh wedja seneb!"
(Peace in the heavens, peace on earth. Life, health, and prosperity!)

Ending the ritual with the breaking of bread seems a suitable way to help the participants to ground themselves after the experiencing the waking of their Netjer. It will also a grant a social element to the experience wherein the ritualists can discuss their experience, any advice received from the Netjer and so on.

Given that this is intended as a morning ritual, it should be balanced with a nocturnal ceremony following a similar pattern but in which the deity is thanked and the cosmetics, and lengths of cloth are removed. At the end of the ritual the doors of the cupboard should be closed and sealed (be that by locking the door, or cording the handles and attaching a wax seal, or by some other method).

Rather than calling the Netjer to awaken, at the end of the day commend him or her to sleep by saying:

Qed Sobek
Qed em hotep!
Qed nefer.
Qed, Qed, Qed!
(Rest Sobek, rest in peace! Rest in beauty, rest, rest, rest!)

Tameran Wicca, a branch of the Craft that draws inspiration from Egypt and takes its name from one of the titles of Egypt Ta-meri, includes Circle casting and the calling upon of the four quarters, often symbolised by the four sons of Heru who guarded the canopic jars into which the organs of the dead were placed – Imsety, Hapi, Duamutef, and Qebehsenuef. None of these features have been included in the above ritual, but could easily be added if it suits the taste of the reader. Reproduction canopic jars of varying sizes can be found from some gift shops. As well as being beautiful things to look at they can be repurposed for ritual, no longer as repositories for organs but for holding granular incense, small amulets, ritual jewellery, and the like. It's a modern fancy, but the ritual practices of Egypt were not static during the history of the pharaohs. They changed and adapted, and there is no reason why devotees in the 21st century cannot do the same.

Ritual Calendar

What we know of the Kemetic calendar is broad but sadly not deep. Almost every other day is ascribed to a festival of some sort, such that no single Egyptian could have realistically celebrated them all and held down a day job at the same time. In some respects, this is comparable to the Catholic calendar with its countless saints' days, the majority of which any given Catholic will largely ignore as they choose instead to focus on the days celebrating only a few of the many saints. It seems equally likely that most inhabitants of the Black Land would have celebrated a small number of festivals peculiar to their town or village and a few nationwide festivities whilst largely ignoring the local festivities peculiar to that town ten miles away. As long as the important festivities were conducted by the clergy, the rest of the population could get on with more immediate concerns.

Very little is known about the details of the majority of festivities beyond their names and rough time of year. This necessitates the 21st century practitioner having to communicate with the entity to which the festival is dedicated to find out what it means and how it is expected to be celebrated. Returning briefly to issue of reconstruction, it is not always possible to ascertain when a given festival was instituted or fell out of practice. As a result, someone wishing to recreate the festival calendar of a specific period (such as the New Kingdom) may not be able to say with any confidence exactly which annual festivities would have been celebrated then. The website of the University College London maintains an excellent resource giving many of the festivals. The reader is directed to the website for full details, rather than attempting to include a list of all known dates here. Instead we will look at some of the nationwide celebrations. Details below are mostly based on the research conducted by Siegfried Schott (1950).

The year opens with the great *heb* (festival) of *Wepet-Renpet*, Opener of the Year, on the first day of Tekh which is dated by the flooding of the Nile, which of course no longer occurs since the building of the Aswan Dam. The flood itself is foreshadowed by the rising of the Dog Star Sirius (*Sopdet* to the Egyptians) which used to happen in early July back in the days of the first dynasties. Astronomical factors have pushed this back to early August these days. There are websites which can calculate the rising of Sirius for any given latitude, which requires a judgement call as to whether to use the date of its rising in Egypt or to use the latitude of your hometown should you not live in Egypt itself. Having seen the star rise, the priests of old fixed *Wepet-Renpet* on the following new moon. Given this fluidity of calendar, the dates of any of the subsequent festivals will shift from year to year. Organising ceremonies will also need to fit around the busy lives that people have these days.

Whatever date is settled on, the next question becomes how to celebrate New Year. The festivity became the birthday of Re-Horakhty in later Egyptian history, following the syncretisation of Re and Heru. It was common practice to bathe in the Nile in the early morning, which could be re-enacted with a dip in the nearest river or the sea itself. Some accounts talk of people pouring black liquids, possibly ink, into the Nile although this seems rather environmentally unfriendly these days. A non-harmful alternative could be substituted to symbolise the flowing away of the night as the sun is reborn. People exchanged gifts, especially ones bearing the hieroglyphic inscription of *wepet-renpet nefert* (roughly, beautiful opener of the year). In the Tale of the Two Brothers the unjustly accused Bana calls upon Re-Horakhty as the Netjer who distinguishes guilt from innocence. This might be a theme suitable for some who wish aid from the divine to vindicate them of unjust accusations. It seems in keeping with a New Year to start with a fresh slate wiped clean of false suspicions. As with New Year festivities the world over,

Wepet-Renpet was marked with plenty of food, drink, music, dancing, and general partying. There are some recipes known from ancient times and it is a nice inclusion for the feasting table to have something from those days to share. Once each temple was built a consecration ceremony took place in which the pharaoh, or perhaps a representative for the minor temples, handed the holy place over to the chief deity who resided in the sacred enclosure. At each New Year this hand-over process was renewed. For those lucky enough to have a permanent shrine, the act of renewal could form part of their *Wepet-Renpet* festivities.

The month of Tekh also features the Festival of Intoxication (perhaps a hair of the dog for those still hungover from New Year) in which the story of the lion goddess Sekhmet and her transformation into Het-Heru (Hathor) is marked. The tale, briefly summarised already in Chapter Two, speaks of Re creating the lioness Sekhmet to purge the wicked from the world. Sekhmet's insatiable hunger frightens people so much they seek to placate her with a lake of beer at Dendera, dyed to resemble blood. After guzzling it she passed out drunk and woke up hours later transmuted into the Netjer of love, the cow Het-Heru. Needless to say, this festival was marked by people drinking themselves under the table with red-dyed beer. If you opt to mark this event it will require a tad more planning – given that participants are likely to be too sozzled to drive home and will need a bed for the night. Not everyone can get safely drunk of course – if they are on certain medications or are recovering alcoholics – and some thought should be given to ways in which they could be included rather than feeling they have to stay at home and skip this *heb*. For those with a talent for brewing, a nice wheat or barley beer could be made a few months ahead and coloured with strawberries, raspberries, or similar fruit. The making of the beer can be dedicated to Tenenet, goddess of the brew, or to Setekh, who is credited with inventing it. If Sekhmet agrees, pomegranate or plum wine could be used instead.

Carolyn Graves-Brown (2010) states that the festival started during the Middle Kingdom but had become unpopular several centuries later before being restored to practice in Roman Egypt, possibly because the Romans had many celebrations of their own which involved heavy drinking. This is worth bearing in mind for modern reconstructionists – the calendar was not static over the millennia and a decision must be made as to which version of the calendar will be celebrated. A Kemeticist could aim for a particular period, such as the Middle Kingdom, or opt to celebrate those festivities associated with whichever of the Netjeru or *akhu* most closely calls to them, even if this means marking festivities that might have been a thousand years or more apart in terms of when they were added to (or dropped from) the calendar.

The *Wag heb* is mentioned in papyri from the Old Kingdom and marks the death of green-skinned Asur. The dating of Wag falls in line with the appearance of Orion in the eastern sky, which usually rises around middle to late August. The Egyptologist von Beckerath places it on the 18th day of the month of Tekh on the civic calendar, which equates with 15th September. This is the time of year when the grapevines would start to ripen, fed by the Nile floodwaters, after having seemed withered and dead. Whether you choose to celebrate by partaking of the previous year's grape harvest depends on how much your liver can take from all this constant partying. It was also the time to honour the *Akhu*, the beloved dead who resided peacefully in the next world. As with similar festivals in other parts of the world, people tended the tombs and graves of their loved ones and left out food offerings for them. One tradition which is easy enough to engage in describes people making toy boats to sail off to the west, where the sun sets and the dead reside with Asur. Paper boats are easy to make and, if they cannot be retrieved will at least mulch into the river bed and cause no pollution issues.

Herodotus tells us that the annual festival of the cat deity

Bast was elaborate and marked with boatloads of people travelling down the Nile. Some women played their sistra, metal rattles that were likely played by swinging them back and forth in unison to create a rhythmic beat, whilst men played flutes. When the boats moored at cities along the way these female musicians went ashore dancing and some engaging in the sort of comedic flashing of their genitals already discussed earlier in the book. In Bubastis itself, cult centre of the cat goddess, the Greek informant claims that more wine was drunk at this one festival than the rest of the year put together. The reader might be forgiven at this juncture for thinking that the Ancient Egyptians must have had serious alcohol problems! Herodotus may be guilty of some hyperbole in his descriptions but, even if he was presenting the unvarnished truth, modern followers need not shrivel their livers if they do not wish to. Wine aside, music and dance could form central features of a modern *heb-Bast*.

Alongside annual festivities it is worth giving some attention to the rites of passage in the life of a *shems* of the old gods. Birth, coming of age, marriage, elderhood, and death are all important events although there is very little evidence for ordinary people marking such events in temples.

The hippopotamus goddess Tuaret was especially favoured by pregnant women as the Netjer to ease the many aches and pains of carrying a child to term. The gift of an amulet, icon, or some other representation of Tuaret is wholly suitable for any pregnant Kemetic. Another Netjer, one of the few with no overt animal associations, Meskhenet also watched over mother and child. It was she who formed the *ka* and bound it to the baby at the moment of birth. It is a point worth noting as it may reflect ancient attitudes towards abortion and miscarriage, as well as potentially influencing the views of modern people. It might be argued that the binding of *ka* to flesh constitutes personhood – how do people comprehend the legal and social standing of the foetus before the binding of the *ka*? At the point of giving birth the frog-headed Heqet took over as the overseer of midwifery.

Modern Egyptians celebrate the *sebou* festival seven days after a child is born. There is no direct mention in ancient papyri of children being named on the seventh day, but his number symbolism plays a significant part in many myths so it is not wholly unlikely. The number seven is significant, and it is traditional to start acquiring toys, a crib, and all the other paraphernalia from the seventh month of pregnancy. Grandparents often present a gift of seven sets of baby clothes. The infant is place in a large kitchen sieve which is gently shaken before being laid on the floor. A grandmother or elderly aunt beats out a rhythm using a pestle and mortar. The female relatives sing a mildly humorous song with instructions to the baby about living a good life, incense is burnt as the mother steps over the child seven times, each step dedicated to Allah. It is argued that whilst this is now part of Muslim rituals peculiar to Egypt, it actually dates back to ancient times where the dedication would have been to other deities. Children join the ceremony by holding candles to lead the mother and new-born around whilst more singing takes place, and eventually the exchange of small gifts. There are no suggestions of any grand baby naming ceremonies taking place in the temples, and it may well have been a wholly domestic affair much like the one practiced by modern Muslims with the child presented to relatives and the name formally announced to all and sundry.

At the beginning of the Inscription of Weni the royal official recollects being a child and fastening on a girdle of his first adult employment. Whether the girdle is just a metaphor or was part of an actual puberty ritual in which the child became an adult is unclear. A variety of cultures mark the transition to adulthood with a change of some item of clothing or jewellery. The dwarf Netjer Bes was regarded as one of the protectors of children, and parents might well want to give their youngsters a Bes pendant which could then be taken off as part of a coming of age rite and maybe stored away to be passed on to other children in the future.

There is evidence of polygamous marriages amongst the very wealthy as well as the monogamous format that most of us are more familiar with. Whilst pharaohs may have engaged in considerable pomp and ceremony for their unions, the majority of people seem to have done little more than formally declare their union before family and friends before living together. Certainly, a cheaper arrangement than the ludicrously expensive weddings we see today. The blessings of the royal couple Aset and Asur might be called upon, though same-sex couples might favour different Netjeru. Which deities should be called upon in the latter case is debatable. Setekh attempts a sexual relationship with Heru in one myth, but as this is an act of incestuous rape it hardly seems appropriate to cast Setekh in the light of a patron of loving gay marriages.

Evidence for how the ancients understood relationships between people of the same sex is scanty. There are suggestive accounts, such as the Pharaoh Pepi II's nocturnal visits to the home of Sasenet, but nothing which is so far definitive. There is strong evidence that adultery was strongly disapproved of for both men and women, which could well have included discouragement of extra-marital affairs with people of the same sex. The Egyptians do not seem to have been overly concerned by the sex lives of the unmarried, which may have included indifference regarding associations between two men or two women.

As Deborah Sweeney (2011) notes, there is scant evidence for any rites associated with the menopause or comparable elderhood in men. Older women hardly appear at all in Egyptian art. This does not mean that there were no such ceremonies nor that modern people might not wish to create their own wholly original ways of marking this stage of life.

When it comes to funerals and mourning Herodotus tells us that the Egyptians, as so often, did things in a reverse manner to many other nations. Whilst in other parts of the world (at least those with which he was familiar) people shaved their hair to signify their state of grief, the normally bald and clean-shaven citizens of the Black Land let their hair and beards grow out. As in 17th century Europe where the gentry kept their natural hair close cropped in order to don elaborate wigs, so those Egyptian men and women who could afford scented wigs kept their scalps shorn presumably to reduce the likelihood of overheating. Later Herodotus goes on to explain that the hairless state is essentially for cleanliness rather than mystical reasons, *"Their priests shave the whole body every other day, so that no lice or anything else foul may infest them as they attend upon the gods."* These days more people around the world have good sanitation to prevent parasites, so it is debatable if depilation is really necessary in the same way. However, some modern Kemetics do like to stick to the old ways on this issue.

Considerable detail exists for the funerals of the rich and prominent, much less about those of ordinary people. It seems unlikely that many modern Kemetics could afford the extravagant rituals associated with pharaohs and viziers. For those who could afford it, embalming was standard. Modern embalming techniques are somewhat different, and there is the ecological impact of using the current array of chemicals on bodies to take into account when arranging funerals. In earlier times a procession of *sem*-priests and mourners (including professional mourners) accompanied the body to the tomb where the Opening of the Mouth ritual took place. This procession was led by two heralds carrying flags bearing the symbols of Wepwawet, the Opener of the Ways. The newly dead person takes the part of Asur in mythology and must be awakened into the afterlife with the Opening of the Mouth and Eyes ceremony described a little further on in this chapter. Two women, probably professional mourners though sometimes they may have been relatives, took the parts of Aset and Neheb-het in welcoming the body to its tomb, the *serdab* (inner sanctum) of which effectively became the place of rebirth into the next world. Modern Wiccans have the ritual of Calling Down the Moon in which a priestess seeks to channel the presence of her goddess, a practice not dissimilar to the forms of spirit possession practiced in Santeria, Candomblé, and similar faiths. What is unclear from the records is whether the women representing the two Netjeret were simply acting, much as a mummer might take the part of Jesus in a Passion play, or if they sought some form of divine possession.

The Egyptian word for widow is *kharet*, the hieroglyph being a lock of hair. Ann Macy Roth (2000) argues that the reason for this is that one of the expressions of mourning for a woman was to cut off some (possibly all) of her hair. The story of Asur's murder includes reference to his widow Aset cutting off a lock of her hair. A number of cultures include hair-related traditions in conjunction with funerals and periods of mourning. Italian women and, up until recently, Irish and Scottish women would cover their hair with a shawl during periods of mourning.

Opening the Mouth and Eyes (*wepet-er*)

The Opening the Mouth ritual first appears in written accounts from the Old Kingdom period. It was used in a variety of contexts centred on the idea of granting speech and consciousness to someone or something that lacked it, such as the recently dead or statues of dead people or deities. When performed on a corpse, the aim was to release the *ba* that it might unite with the *ka* and so form the basis of the *akh*. Over the course of centuries, the rite changed and varied, so there is no singular one correct form that has to be used. A detailed account of this rite was found carved into a wall in the Theban tomb of Rekhmire, dating back to the 18th Dynasty.

The body or statue was placed upon a mound of sand,

symbolic of the *benben* that emerged from the sea of chaos. Four *nemsetu*, jars of fresh water, were emptied over the body or statue whilst invoking the name of Heru to cleanse it both physically and spiritually. Incense, natron, and kohl were used in a manner reminiscent of the morning ritual to awaken a sacred statue described earlier on in this chapter. A funeral priest would play the role of the corpse and, at a key juncture in the proceedings, spring back to life. For the funeral of an important military figure, animal sacrifices would be offered so that their blood would represent the vital fluids of any enemies. The ethics of animal sacrifice from a 21st century perspective are hotly debated. In some countries (such as the UK) the act is illegal and the majority of people would find it deeply offensive – even if they are omnivores who would happily munch on a bacon sandwich. In other parts of the world it is legal, though usually regulated such that only certain people with a degree of training can carry out the killing competently. In some parts of the world the animal is cooked and eaten afterwards as part of a religious feast. The killing of another creature, whether for the dinner plate or any other reason, is not an act to be undertaken lightly or by the unskilled.

The *tekenu* is a somewhat mysterious figure that has been interpreted in different ways. In various examples of wall art, the *tekenu* is little more than a lump wrapped up in what may be a bull hide. The unformed nature of the lump could be the offal or "left-overs" removed from the corpse in the evisceration process but which were not placed in canopic jars. The series of images in Rekhmire's tomb suggests to Reeder (1995) and others that actually this was a priest (in the majority of depictions the *tekenu* has a human face) in a state of trace that would awake at the end of the rite, returning from a shamanic trip to commune with the discarnate soul of the dead. The lump might be better understood as the priest curled into a foetal position, covered in the hide much as Irish *filidh* and druids are described as doing during the *tarbh-feis* ceremony to find the future monarch. The hide may be a means of inducing trance through the combination of darkness and weight. The animal skin used in the Irish example was straight off the dead bull, and quite likely extremely pungent (if you have ever scrapped the fat from an animal hide, the stench is indescribable). A number of modern pagans engage in soul-midwifery, using shamanic and other techniques to aid the dying to pass over smoothly. The role of the *tekenu* would appear to fit well with this practice.

Several objects are used as part of the ceremony, including the *an-heru*, an incense holder shaped like an outstretched arm with an open hand. The *peseshkaf* is a curiously shaped blade commonly made out of obsidian, the sharpened end of which splits into two curved sections vaguely reminiscent of flower petals or a fish tail. Scenes depicting the use of these objects during the ritual can be found on papyri and other artworks. The *peseshkaf* was also used by midwives to cut the umbilical cord, and so echoes birth into this world with birth into another. It may be the case that the blade was used to cut a pretend umbilical cord, such as a rope tied around the body or statue (though quite what the other end was attached to is not a matter that can currently be answered, but presumably something that was actually or metaphorically the mother).

The *ur-hekau* is a blade or wand shaped like a serpent, commonly made out of semi-precious red stone such as carnelian. If the modern practitioner wishes to include such implements on their altar, then a carved carnelian may prove prohibitively expensive and it is recommended to substitute a cheaper material that has been painted red and maybe has an easily affordable small piece of carnelian set into it.

A device somewhat like an adze blade, called a *setep* or *meskhetyu*, was also used along with the *nua*, which resembles an index and middle finger conjoined and could easily be made out of clay or similar material. The adze-like instrument was passed across the mouth and eyelids of the body or statue to symbolically open them up. The adze is one of the tools associated with Wepwawet, as the great opener of things that have been sealed. The *sem*-priest touches the lips of the dead with his fingertips, an act crystallised in the finger amulet.

Much of the *Weret-er* ceremony took place in the presence of stone masons and labourers who would adjust statues and move hefty objects about as the priests chanted, intoned august phrases, and so forth.

Miniature versions of these items were included as amulets in burials, wrapped up in the mummification cloth. For those wishing to wear such amulets in modern ceremony, they can either be made at home or ordered through specialist shops and artisans, as can the full-sized versions. It must be born in mind that these replicas are rarely made from the same materials the originals were, but are formed from other materials that are more accessible and usually cheaper. Some of these articles will be returned to in Chapter Ten.

Once the Opening was complete the *akh* of the dead person would come into existence and be able to see, eat offerings, speak, and generally able to use their newly opened mouth and eyes. Rosalie David (2002) suggests that the reason for the elaborate artwork inside tombs, which none of the painters ever expected to be witnessed by the living once the door was sealed, was that it too was believed to come to life so that the newly animated soul could enjoy the flowers, animals, hunting scenes and such like. The Opening of the Mouth and Eyes may have brought a great deal more to life than a single corpse or statue. Magical paintings could be created by the modern Kemetic to decorate their sacred spaces, created with the intent that ancestors, deities, or other spirits be able to live within the artworks once the ceremony has awakened them to life.

Likewise, a statue that had been Opened could engage in eating, watching and so on in a manner that has echoes to the

Jewish concept of the golem. Jewish scholars continue to debate the exact origins of the golem legends, but this prominent folkloric figure is a creature of clay brought to a form of life by cabalistic magic centred on the use of gematria, magical words and numbers. It may be that gematria originated in Egypt as a concept and was adapted to the Hebrew alphabet. Most golem legends describe these creatures as being manufactured to act as servants or bodyguards. They can follow simple instructions and, in some cases, such as the golem of Prague, demonstrate fairly complex reasoning in protecting the ghetto community from the evil machinations of characters like Brother Thaddeus. The one capacity that seems to distinguish Egyptian from Hebrew concepts is the capacity to speak. Having had life breathed into it, the golem invariably lacks the power of speech. The link between the golem and the *shabti* statuettes that jump to life in the world beyond to carry out menial work for the soul in bliss seems clear.

Chapter Five

Ethics and Philosophy

The main source of information about the kinds of ethical guidelines taught by exponents of Egyptian religion is the Declaration of Innocence already mentioned in Chapter Three. As a supplement to this there are also a number of papyri in which one person gives advice on living a good life to another, such as the Instructions of Ptahhotep. To begin this chapter, we will review some of the ideas of the past, but to close it we will consider how these apply to the present. As with any religion with a degree of antiquity, the way things were done centuries or millennia earlier is not necessarily the way people would wish to do them now. We must also factor in developments in technology that pose moral challenges which simply did not exist for our distant ancestors and whose moral values may therefore be of limited use. Reflecting on aged texts is fascinating and worthwhile, but it does not automatically answer all questions in the present.

The Egyptians, like virtually all ancient cultures, placed tremendous importance on family and loyalty between kin. Having no welfare state, it was primarily the job of family to take care of their own. The Tale of Two Brothers somewhat suggests that blood should triumph over the ties of marriage, in that the moral failure of the elder brother Anpu is to trust his dishonest wife over his devoted younger sibling. He is so convinced by her accusation against his brother that he is prepared to murder Bata without asking to hear a word of denial or self-defence.

The unnamed wife engages in *isfet* by subverting the natural order of things – she lusts after the youth that she has previously treated like a son. Whilst marital incest may have been practiced amongst the royal families (whether these were marriages in

110

name alone, or if there was an expectation of sex is unclear), amongst the poorer sections of society this seems to have been regarded as disordered. This issue of subversion is a challenging one for modern readers and practitioners, in that a great deal of what we now enjoy in the west (and, indeed, many parts of the east) is the result of political change and social upheaval. If our fairly recent ancestors had not revolted against the existing political order of their day then many of us might be slaves, or unable to vote or own property, or be sending our children up chimneys or into incredibly dangerous factories, mine shafts etc. There are still plenty of parts of the world in which people still suffer these problems but, perhaps swept along on the wave of Canadian psychologist Steven Pinker's enthusiasm for the 21st century, it is possible to see the day soon arriving when they too will be freed from such oppressive horrors. When their freedom dawns it will also be because of people bucking the system.

Egyptian morality favoured stability, continuity, respect for power structures, and many of what we tend to label as conservative values in this age. There is something of a challenge in squaring the benefits of social revolution with an ethical system that inclines to preserving traditions. Canadian psychologist and philosopher Jordan Peterson, explores the idea of two political trends (he speaks in terms of the left-wing and the right-wing, but the concepts can still apply to cultures where these terms are not used) where the more conservative one builds up hierarchies, structures, divisions of labour, and so forth. The more liberal or progressive trend is more inclined to critique the hierarchies and social forms, pointing out where they do not work or produce unwanted side-effects. Peterson argues that a society which only generates structures quickly becomes fossilised, whilst one that only tears them down will descend into chaos – both are needed for balance and constructive growth. One could see here an echo to *ma'at* and *isfet*, except that what Peterson is really describing is a move towards a positive society that creates social structures and then reviews them to find means of improvement. Both the constructing and reviewing are ultimately *ma'at*, both needed for a healthy culture. One alone creates imbalance. The social upheavals which dispensed with slavery, brought full citizenship to men and women regardless of social class, and so forth might well have shocked Ancient Egyptians (especially the conflict and discord that brought about the changes), but are part of this process of improving structures that had become suffocating and rigid.

Whilst the Netjeru are the essence of *ma'at*, the manifestation of *isfet* is the giant serpent-demon Apepi. Whilst some modern writers are wont to describe Setekh as a devil-like figure, making analogies to Christianity, it is really the great snake that is more akin to Satan. In fact, it is worth noting that the red god is an active enemy of the serpent and defends Ra on the journey through the underworld. Though a dangerous force, there were a couple of monarchs who named themselves after Apepi. He bears the title World Encircler, very reminiscent of the vast snake Jormungardr that appears in Scandinavian myth as an opponent of the gods of Asgard. Just as the Norse world serpent was blamed for causing earthquakes, so Apepi was seen as responsible for at least some natural evils in the world – particularly drought and the famines that it would lead to. The failure of sufficient floodwaters to fertilise the land were seen as the result of Apepi guzzling the waters.

An effigy of the Lord of Chaos was burnt every year in a festival somewhat akin to Guy Fawkes Night. The source of wickedness in the world is worth reflecting on a little. Jan Assmann, perhaps influenced by Judeo-Christian notions of the Fall, tracks it back to the rebellion of humanity against Re which, amongst other things, results in the emergence of wrathful Sekhmet to consume the sinful. The Cosmogony of Esna accounts for Apepi emerging from the umbilical cord of Re, which could lend itself to a quasi-Freudian interpretation that the serpent-cord pulls him back towards the primordial soup of Nun whose formlessness is surely the ultimate source of chaos. What Budge (and other subsequent writers) saw as malevolent forces in the service of Setekh, the *mesu badesh*, also seek to overthrow divine order and wallow in the resultant disarray. This view sees *isfet* as integral to the cosmos rather than as something emerging consequent to wicked behaviour. The idea of discordant forces as being fundamental to the fabric of the world is also found in the cabalistic understanding of the Qlippoth, the Tree of Death, which is sometimes described as being like the slag produced as a result of refining metals from ore. The wicked qualities of the Qlippoth are a natural waste product in the process of creation. It may well be that many ideas now current within cabalism can trace their roots to Egyptian influences.

The 'Book of Overthrowing Apepi' is essentially a set of exorcism rituals rather than a moral guide for overcoming the evil within oneself. Purification plays a strong role in Kemetic ritual, and a sense can be gleaned of the need to effectively repent of wrongdoing (in the heart, if not necessarily in a public display of chest beating). The *Ru Nu Peret Em Heru*, the Book of the Dead also called the Book of Coming Forth by Day, contains Spell 14 which is to be said to remove anger form the heart of a deity. Why the Netjer is angry is not made clear, but as the deceased soul is on a journey of atonement and preparation for entry into the fields of the blessed it seems not unreasonable to suppose that this may have been a formula for seeking forgiveness from a deity for some offence made against them. The words and accompanying offering make a suitable prayer for anyone contemplating things they have done wrong and wishing for a fresh start. Faulkner's translation is given here:

"Hail to you who descend in power, chief of all secret matters!
Behold my word is spoken: so says the god who was angry with me.
Wrong is washed away, and it falls immediately. O Lords of Justice,

may this god be gracious to me, may my evil be removed for you. O Lord of Offerings, as mighty ruler, behold I have brought to you a propitiation-offering so that you may live in it and that I may live on it; be gracious to me and remove all anger which is in your heart against me."

A question arises regarding injured people. If the Netjer who has been offended must be offered a gift, then must amends also be made towards any humans or other beings harmed (be they living or dead)? A culture in which restitution is made towards those harmed seems greatly preferable to one in which the victims of wrongdoing are shrugged off and ignored simply because some prayers have been said. There may well be occasions in which those who have been ill-used can no longer be found or, even if they are found, wish to have no contact with the offender and outright refuse any compensation offered them. At such times as these, the genuinely repentant heart which has learnt why former actions were wrong can still seek a fresh start. As a suggestion, the offering that would have been made to the victim can still be made but directed towards a substitute source – maybe given to a suitable charity, or something of the sort as an act of restitution.

The Declaration is not a direct cognate to the Ten Commandments handed down on Sinai, but it is certainly a deontological system by which moral decisions can be made. Moral relativism would probably not have sat well with the Egyptians, with its ultimate lack of strong rules to order life by.

Rather than giving an in-depth analysis of all the statements of the Declaration, which would easily fill a book in itself, let us gloss through most and consider just a handful of them in greater degree. Quite a few of these moral statements relate to agricultural communities and establish patterns that would encourage good neighbourliness. Others relate to exhibiting respect for the temples and their property, which in some ways seem to imply similar resentments as those felt by many European peasants had towards the enormously wealthy monasteries whose crops, livestock, and so forth must have tempted many an impoverished yokel. The Papyrus of Nu likewise contains a lot of moral injunctions centred on agriculture. Agriculture is still hugely important (few people would choose to starve to death)

Some of those listed in the Papyrus of Ani are fairly straightforward such as the second statement: I have not committed robbery with violence. This clearly applies as much to bank robbers in the 21st century as to highway bandits 5000 years ago. On a similar theme of larceny, the fifth statement (I have not stolen grain) can simply be taken as something that is largely left in the past – given that very few people probably steal grain these days. Though that may show my complacent first world bias, and maybe in parts of the world where famine is a major issue there are plenty of people purloining sacks of corn or wheat. Or it could be taken as a modern metaphor for not taking the food out of other people's mouths, not taking from people the basics of their survival regardless of what type of food it might be. The subsequent confession, I have not purloined offerings, obviously refers to taking things donated to a temple but could quite reasonably be generalised out to items gifted in any spiritual context and regardless of religion ~ such as flowers left at a grave, money given to the church poor box, or a sword cast into the waters at a druidic site. This later raises some curious thoughts because stealing is not a totally clear-cut action. If an archaeologist unearths a golden statuette of Bast and donates it to a museum, few people would class it as theft. Yet a person has taken something that is not theirs from a place where it had been deliberately left, and they have disposed of it. Waltzing off with your neighbour's garden gnome and donating it to a charity shop could result in the police being called. The fact that you have not kept the gnome nor sold it for personal profit does not make the action legal. The major difference in these two examples is, of course, that the neighbour is still alive whilst the owner of the Bast statuette is long dead and not in a position to complain. How we handle ancient religious offerings is often different from the way we treat contemporary ones, much as our treatment of the recently dead differs from that of the antique dead. The seventh point seems quite similar to the sixth, so we might assume that the property of the God must have been something other than offerings made by devotees. Possibly it may have been such things as the fixtures and fittings of the temple and so a warning against the ancient equivalent of stealing the lead off the church roof.

The eleventh exhortation to avoid adultery echoes the twentieth against debauching of a married woman, though perhaps these concepts were understood differently. As mentioned in the previous chapter, the focus on the stability of family was such that anything which undermined the trust between spouses was disapproved of. An area for personal reflection here would be on the matter of open relationships – if the extra-marital relationship is conducted with consent of the spouse, does it still constitute adultery? For many religions the answer to that would be yes, however someone choosing to follow the Declaration will need to decide for themselves how to interpret the definition of this particular impermissible behaviour. Debauching may have been understood as something other than adultery.

The thirteenth instruction about eating the heart is obviously not one about cannibalism, but might be taken to refer to the kind of all-consuming jealousy that Shakespeare alludes to when talking about the green-eyed monster that mocks the meat on which it feeds. To allow oneself to be become bitter and twisted is dangerous, particularly where invidia takes hold – the Roman word for that state of mind where people so resent others having what they cannot that they seek to destroy what the other has. It is this mentality that has led many people to murder their spouses rather than allow them to go off and be happy with someone else. It is the sort of attitude that declares, if I cannot have someone or something then nobody else shall be allowed to have it either. Bear in mind that the *ab* is not only the emotional core which the heart represents in modern semiotics, but the mind and conscience in general.

The warning not to attack any man (or presumably woman) might be taken to refer to the instigation of violence against the innocent, since the Egyptians were clearly in favour of self-defence. It may be taken as a rebuke against instigating needless violence, where a problem could have either been ignored or resolved by more peaceful means. A question arises as to whether attack should be understood in a purely physical sense or if it would extend to verbal abuse or even magical or psychical attacks.

The eighteenth statement against slander perhaps builds on this potential idea of verbal assaults and would extend to libel in this widely literate era, and is something we might well reflect on as especially relevant given the degree to which social media enables ordinary people to spread false rumours even more readily than can the sleaziest of tabloid journalists.

The twentieth and twenty-first seem to abjure the same thing. Debauching here may be read simply as having sex, or more psychologically in the sense of trying to corrupt another person – inducing a hatred of their spouse where none previously existed perhaps. Although the wording speaks about debauching the wife, a modern reader might equally take it that trying to have the same effect on someone's husband would be just as bad.

The twenty-second rejection of self-pollution has provoked discussion amongst translators, who are sometimes more influenced by the moral values of their own day than those of Egypt. Suggestions as to what constitutes pollution in this sense have included masturbation, homosexual activity, and paedophilia. The Black Nationalist movement which is mostly focused in America tends to be very hostile to same-sex attraction, often denouncing it as against *ma'at* and portraying it (in very unhistorical fashion) as a white man's "sin". Quite a lot of these Nationalists are adherents of Kemeticism and use the word *hotep* as a greeting, which has led to critics of the movements to refer to them mockingly as hotepians. Some may regard this view of homosexuality as valid; others may see it as a very modern and insecure macho swagger that fails to understand the sexual mores of the ancient world (let alone the modern one). It may be something of a modern-day projection to read pollution in this context as necessarily being some activity of a sexual nature. Quite how the reader chooses to take it may reflect as much about their existing morality as an attempt to embrace whatever the values of millennia past might have been or of the Netjeru still are.

The witness borne before Shet-kheru is most likely a rejection of unnecessary anger or ill-temper rather than the righteous anger that might be felt towards injustice or wickedness. The subsequent refusal to shut one's ears to the words of truth might be interpreted in the light of judicial matters, in the sense of listening to denouncements of the wicked rather than pretending that nothing is happening. Alternatively, it might be seen as keeping open to spiritual truths.

The thirty-third statement that one has wronged none nor done any evil seems so broad as to do away with the need for any of the other declarations. However, the term evil might be understood as something quite specific, perhaps sadism or torture. The following rebuttal of witchcraft should not be taken as a rejection of Wicca, but clearly relates to the use of magical acts for seditious purposes to undermine the monarch. Faulkner's translated list gives a similar sentiment as the thirty-fifth declaration. Both before and after the election of the American president Donald Trump assorted pagans declared via social media that they would be using their magical skills to either prevent his passage to the White House (which clearly failed) or to cause his impeachment. Pagans in other parts of the world may also have used less well publicised magic to attempt to get rid of their political leaders. A question arises as to how we understand the nature of the pharaoh in the modern world. Do moral injunctions such as the thirty-fourth one apply only historically to a political office no longer in existence, or should modern Kemetics apply them to whoever sits in the role of political leader of their homeland? If the moral guidelines are updated and broadened out to apply to countries other than Egypt itself, then potentially it might be considered unethical to utilise magic to undermine an existing leader (though trying to prevent someone from becoming leader would not seem to violate this particular restriction). Yet there are no shortage of examples of monstrous tyrants whose removal would have been a great benefit to their citizens and neighbours. Is it so wrong to use what means sit at hand to try and neutralise such a monster? That said, lovers of democracy might well suggest that it is much better to depose a tyrant openly through the ballot box than through furtive acts of sorcery.

An alternate approach to thirty-four is to consider some other person than a nation's leader to have the role of pharaoh. As mentioned in the first chapter, the Kemetic Orthodox religious movement is led by Dr Tamara Siuda who bears the title of Nisut, or pharaoh, which is indicative that some people may look to non-political figures as having the function of pharaoh and so deserving of suitable ethical treatment. There are, of course, various other branches of Egyptian religion which have no living pharaoh and for whom figures such as Dr Siuda have no leadership role.

The forty-first rule speaks of not being contemptuous towards the deity of the deceased's city. Whilst this is fairly straightforward it does have an angle of interest in the light of Roman theology. The Romans believed in the *lars praestites*, the guardian spirits of each city or smaller settlements. Each town or city had its own spirit that had to be duly respected. The concept has carried over into Christianity with its patron saints of every country and many cities, such as St Piran who watches over Cornwall, St Titus who looks after Crete, and St Barbara of Syria. Alongside whichever Netjeru a person might be drawn to at different stages in life, the suggestion here is that they should also be on good terms with whoever looks after the place in which they live. For those living outside of Egypt this may well be a deity or other being who is not a member of the Egyptian pantheon.

Faulkner's list includes concepts which do not appear in Budge's translation, such as the eighteenth which mentions not taking part in vexatious litigation, and the fortieth declaration in which the soul protests that they have made no biased judgements (such as in court cases) in their own favour. This latter reflects the notion of the protestations being tailored for the individual – given that a humble farm labourer would never be in a position to subvert the legal system to their own advantage and so would scarcely have need to make such a claim. This list is also more explicit in its condemnation of the pederastic abuse of children as a thing which no decent soul should do.

Given the variations on the Declaration that existed in ancient times, it becomes unwise to select a single version and treat it as being a divinely revealed set of Commandments for modern Kemetics. Rather, it is better to treat the various versions as inspiration and guidelines for the sort of values important in the distant past and which could sagely inform how we live today. In the text following on from the Declaration the newly deceased is recorded as stating their innocence and goodness in other terms including, "*I gave bread to the hungry, water to the thirsty, clothing to the naked, and a ferryboat to him who was marooned.*" Numerous religious texts from the world over espouse sentiments like this and, if followed through, serve as a clear guide for the Kemetic to aid those who are in need. As the saying goes, when you have abundance build a longer table, not a higher fence.

Ethical values can, to some extent, be divined by looking at legal codes, although there is not a complete overlap between the two. Women enjoyed a degree of legal protection in sympathy with the modern liberal outlook and rare in the rest of the world at that point in history. Diodorus records that:

> *"The laws concerning women were very severe. Anyone who was convicted of raping a free woman had to have his genitals cut off; because they considered that this crime included in itself three very great evils: insult, corruption of morals, and confusion of offspring."*

A number of other statements made by Diodorus regarding Egyptian laws have proved to be true, which adds a little to the likelihood that this too may be accurate. Whilst no detailed codex of Egyptian law has yet been discovered, there are piles of documents dealing with trials and the like which make it clear that the people of ancient times objected to most of the same activities that most other nations continue to object to today ~ murder, robbery, defamation of character, welching on legal contracts etc. Alongside this were crimes we are less familiar with in this era, such as tomb robbing. Diodorus' inclusion of the word free is a reminder that enslaved women (and men) had far fewer legal protections and those actions which would be criminal if carried out on a free person might be seen as quite permissible on a slave. We can delude ourselves that slavery no longer exists in the 21st century. It may no longer be legal, but it still goes on and there are additionally categories of people who may not be enslaved per se but who are only a tiny step removed from that state and often subject to appalling treatment that would cause public outrage if inflicted on a person of higher legal status.

Punishments were somewhat more draconian than are to

be expected today (at least in the West), including prolonged floggings, the amputation of various body parts, and execution. Probably few modern people would want to return to that system. Perhaps of more interest may be the idea of courts being run within each town by the *senu*, or circle of elders, whose job it was to maintain a variety of services including law and order. If the *senu* were unable to come to an agreement on a given case, it could be referred upwards to the *kenbet*, regional courts. These courts do not seem to have composed of people with specialist legal training, though they may have been advised by experts on law. To some extent the *senu* reflect the importance of community justice, that each village or town take care of its own problems. On the positive side this would likely mean that members of a *senu* were familiar with the plaintiff and accused, aware of all sorts of issues that enabled them to reach a fair decision. On the other hand, it could doubtless lead to a lot of partiality and bias.

The previously mentioned Instructions of Ptahhotep is regarded as one of the earliest philosophical texts, dating back to around 2540BCE. An extremely elderly sage who serves as adviser to the pharaoh Isesi dispenses wisdom to the son who is soon to inherit his position in the royal court.

One of the things that Ptahhotep rails against is avariciousness, decrying it as a disease that eats away at family loyalties. Anyone who has ever been in involved in a family dispute over an inheritance will probably be in full accord with the aged vizier. He also emphasises the need for truthfulness and calm, measured speech especially in response to the anger of others. Whilst the old man is most likely advising on the best way of dealing with stroppy, ill-tempered royals this can be taken as sage advice for life in general. Similar views can be seen in Jesus' sermon from the mount when he suggests turning the other cheek and so effectively meeting wrath with gentleness rather than trying to fight fire with fire.

Interestingly he also opposes social snobbery to the self-made man (or woman, by extension). People of humble birth who have made the best use of their skills to rise up should be given due respect. For those of a socialist disposition most of this text is likely to rile, given that it thoroughly approves of the aristocratic order of society. It is this one note of social opportunity that may appeal to the politically radical. Hard work, diligence, honesty, and diplomacy are the watchwords for the elderly vizier.

The Instructions of Kagemni, probably written sometime around 2613BCE, has many similar sentiments to Ptahhotep. He is particularly repelled by gluttony and the inability to control appetite, much as was Epicurus many centuries later. Both philosophers are of the opinion that the good things in life are best enjoyed in moderation and that over-indulgence is a sign of weakness. This guideline is unlikely to be a very popular one these days where excess is increasingly the norm. The poetic Proverbs of Amenemope also advise against being a Man of Heat, which is someone who is a slave to their own passions and appetites. The Heated Man is one who is particularly given to stroppy, aggressive attention-seeking scenes and vexatious posturing. At risk of alienating some readers, the western world in the 21st century has a significant number of people whose constant protesting and demands that the wider world change to meet their wishes would undoubtedly have struck Amenemope as the very sort of characters he advised his son against. The modern Kemeticist may take the advice of Amenemope with a pinch of salt – he was, after all, just one more philosopher expressing an opinion and not some oracle of the Divine. However, his views are quite representative of many texts written by the educated and wealthy. As such they may not reflect the moral or political outlooks of the commoner who might well have been more sympathetic to the noisy troublemaker demanding greater rights. The modern reader is best advised to take such Maxims in context and consider how much of them to follow. The first few of the guidelines are one which all people would benefit from following;

> *"Beware of stealing from a destitute man*
> *And of raging against the cripple.*
> *Do not stretch out your hand to touch [harm] an old man,*
> *Nor snipe at the words of an elder.*
> *Don't let yourself be involved in a fraudulent business"*

It continues on, concurring with the advice to be restrained in speech, to sleep on provocative conversations rather than leaping to intemperate responses, to avoid dishonesty in business dealings (such as land-grabbing), and many similar sentiments which are also to be found in the Declaration of Innocence. The recommendation to "not exert yourself to seek out excess/ And your wealth will prosper for you" indicates a sense of *shai* or destiny in which those who are meant to prosper will do so without needing to relentlessly pursue wealth. Addicted gamblers and those who have lost fortunes on the stock market may see the wisdom in this. It also carries a philosophy familiar to Buddhists, Quakers, and others that the truly rich person is one who is content with having just enough for their needs and is not perpetually envious of such luxuries as their neighbours have. Simple contentment brings its own kind of prosperity and is rewarded by the gods.

Another interesting philosophical poem from the Middle Kingdom, 'A Dispute between a Man and his Ba', has been interpreted by some as a strong stance against suicide and by others as more a general warning against despair. The nameless man at the heart of the poem bewails the awfulness of life though it is not wholly clear (some of the text is missing) if he is contemplating suicide or merely wishing death would hurry up and take him. His miseries are in no small part measured by the horrible behaviour of the people around him ~ *"Kindness is perished, insolence assaults everyone"*. The text emerges from the reign of Amenemhet I when the followers of Asur had achieved great prominence and were instituting reforms in theology and ritual. The poem may well have been a performance piece intended to be heard all around Egypt as a means of explaining new ideas and getting people on board with them.

The debate about the nature of evil has gone on for millennia and will doubtless continue for many thousands of years to come. There is no official Kemetic view on what makes someone wicked in the modern sense or wallow in *isfet* in the ancient sense. However, this author would like to add a personal view without any attempt to suggest this is one held by any philosophers in ancient Egypt. The German-American psychologist Erich Fromm first used the term malignant narcissism in 1964, building on concepts laid down by the Hungarian Sándor Ferenczi several decades earlier. Both of them saw infants as passing through a natural state of narcissism where everything is seen from their own view with no understanding of or care about anybody else. A child growing up in a healthy environment will learn to rein this self-fixation in, understand and care about others in turn, develop a capacity to compromise, and so forth. Parents, older siblings, and other people are key in teaching the child to love others and care for them. Some children, however, are very indulged and spoilt by doting parents who seldom if ever say no to any of the child's wishes. The child grows larger, their demands become more unreasonable, and their capacity to cope with being thwarted (on the rare occasions when that happens) remains at the level of infantile petulance. A key factor is that, for this behavioural and psychological pattern to persist into adulthood, others must collude with it. If the parents are no longer around to indulge their spoilt brat, then other people must take on this role to keep the pattern reinforced. Not all thinkers have seen infants as egotists. Jean-Jacques Rousseau, despite being a dreadful hypocrite when it came to his own domestic life, believed humans were innately kind and wonderful. Those benevolent impulses have to be reinforced – where they are persistently ignored or ridiculed or punished, they will start to dwindle and the previously kindly child will turn into something quite unpleasant.

The world of politics is neck deep in examples of self-obsessed adults who have little or no care for others and who respond to being denied with sometimes spectacular displays of rage. Political tyrants can only exist because they are surrounded by sycophants who enable them to be monsters. Wickedness and extreme *isfet* may appear to centre in the terrible behaviour of one person, however they are only able to achieve free reign because so many other people permit them to. People enable abusive behaviour for all sorts of reasons – sometimes kowtowing out of fear, or as a means of currying favour, or because they enjoy joining in with brutality and cruelty, or because the excesses of one-person help cover up their own smaller-scale misdeeds. There are dozens of other motives for joining in, including a rather misguided sense of love that confuse indulgence with affection.

Benevolence and *ma'at* are collectively supported. The saintly, pro-social person is the way they are in part because so many people of a similar temperament have supported them in their path. Likewise, the political or domestic tyrant, the serial killer, child molester, or Reality TV star becomes as extreme as they are because they are helped along the way by people who support them rather than challenge or block them. Rather than centring virtue and vice entirely in individuals, it is more constructive to consider the ways in which we all help to influence and shape the moral character of other people. This is by no means a modern stance, but reflects how the Egyptians and many other ancient peoples thought.

Chapter Six

Magic

The spoken magic of *heka* and the related concept of *renu*, the sacred names of things, have already been mentioned a number of times. The sung or intoned magical words require practice to live them, make them a part of the practitioner's psyche. Dictionaries of Ancient Egyptian words with approximations of their pronunciations are now available to enable the devotee to construct phrases that can be chanted. The development of this form of magic or spiritual development technique is one that needs practice and experimentation. The words to be found in the dictionaries represent the daily language of an ancient people, not necessarily the hidden language for use in the temples.

The Egyptians made extensive use of magic, with numerous examples of wands, talismans, amulets, and various other articles filling the display cabinets of museums the world over. Their understanding of what constituted magic was largely centred on methods of petitioning for divine intervention. A number of ritual objects are mentioned in another chapter, but there are also a few others which the reader might want to consider in terms of whether they have any relevance to their ritual practice.

The *hedj* is a ritual mace, essentially a long wooden handle with a rounded head shaped rather like a lemon. Quite how it was used is unclear, though a mace is clearly a weapon used for coshing enemies and so it may have been used in military as a tool for crushing enemies. Hopefully fairly few readers will have people in their lives that they wish to smite with a mace, so this idea could be applied in the same way that Sufis understand the greater jihad as the quest to overcome one's own sinful, destructive nature (rather than a fight against external political opponents). Overcoming one's own inner demons or personal failings is a valuable task engaged in by adherents of many religions, and the *hedj* could be used as a meditational object for this purpose. Ritual could also be devised the crux of which is the smashing of some clay representation of these dark impulses. Currently translated sources do not give instructions regarding the making or consecration of the *hedj* (or any of the other objects to be mentioned here), so the reader will have to innovate.

Another potential sacred object to consider is a *was*-sceptre, examples of which can be seen being held my many statues. The *was* is a long staff (usually the same height as the statues, so the reader could aim for something roughly their own body length), the top end is curved into the dog-like head of a *nehes* creature whilst the bottom is two slightly curved prongs. Whilst all sorts of deities are depicted holding this sceptre, the *nehes* creature makes it particularly connected to Setekh. There is some suggestion that the design might be based upon a shepherd's crook used in herding flocks.

The word *was* means dominion and the staff was carried to represent authority and command. In terms of practical usage in a 21st century ceremony the sceptre could be used to donate leadership, such that whoever is coordinating a given ritual could be the one to hold the instrument. It could potentially be used to direct the *sekhem* of an individual or group to project a command out into the world. It could also be potentially used in any kind of exorcism where control of a rebellious spirit is required.

Should a *heb* for Asur be conducted then a *heka* and *nekhakha* (crook and flail) could be used to decorate the altar and as devotional objects for him. The *heka* can be seen to represent the king's role as shepherd of the people, whilst the *nekhakha* brings fertility to the land. Were blessings to be required for farmland or a garden then the latter object could be carried round the area to be made fecund. The *heka* might potentially be deployed as a means to bless livestock.

An understanding of magic involves, in part, awareness of the nature of the human being. Several texts describe the multi-layered nature of humanity (it may be that other species were also considered to be composed of all or some of these parts, but this is not clear from the translated works). The exact number of parts does vary from one papyrus to another, but nine is commonly given and it is this number of interacting parts that will be explored here. At other points in Egyptian history the number was considered to be five parts or seven parts. Freud coined the term psychodynamic, and one might well say that the Egyptian system describes a dynamic interaction between the various constituent aspects of the psyche. Unfortunately for us the texts on this topic are somewhat minimal and do not give a full flavour of exactly how the distant inhabitants of Kemet conceived of these spiritual constructs. The minimalism may be because some knowledge was just widely assumed to exist, or considered too sacred to write down, or perhaps the whole issue may have been a matter of dispute that even the philosophers of Kemet could not agree on. There is also the possibility that the key texts with this information have just not been found or translated yet.

1) The Ka is the abstract personality of the individual to whom it belongs. It was considered to be a true reflection of the personality, so perhaps almost like the picture of Dorian Gray and reflective of moral character. The *ka* derives nourishment from food offerings made by mourners, absorbing goodness from the food rather than outright eating it. The *ka* is breathed into the flesh at the moment of birth by (depending on tradition) the goddess Heqet or Meskhenet. The *ka* has the power to enter tomb paintings and to enjoy the scenes and use the false doors as they come to life. After death it remains near the corpse – for the wealthy who could afford one, it lived in the statue of the deceased. In some respects, it is similar to Western ideas of an astral body that becomes a ghost-like presence after death.

2) The *Khat* is the mortal body, our standard flesh and blood. After death this may rot or be preserved accordingly.

3) The *Ba* is the soul, usually depicted as a human-headed bird in art. It contains the instinctual parts of humanity – the sort of impulses and urges centred in the reptilian hindbrain. The Opening of the Mouth ceremony liberated the *ba* from the dead body so it could unite with the *ka* and form the *akh* (assuming, of course, it was able to pass the Declaration of Innocence and enter into the Fields of Aalu as a shining one).

4) The *Ab* is located in the heart within the body, and supplies the vital energy that keeps us ticking. There are similarities to Aristotle's later notion of the nutritive plant soul, the sensitive animal soul, and the rational human soul. The ab is the seat of morality, conscience, and intellect. The weighing of the ab in the halls of judgement reflects the idea that *ma'at* deed would keep the heart light, whilst *isfet* ones would weigh it down.

5) The *Kaibit* or *Shuet* is the shadow cast by the body although it is capable of moving independently from it. Many cultures believe the shadow to be a thing of substance rather than the simple absence of light. A modern reading tends to associate this with the Jungian concept of the Shadow, the dark side of the self. However, this may not be exactly what the Egyptians meant.

6) The *Akh* is the spirit, the divine spark that lives forever and transcends the individual mind of the *ka*. The *akh* is created when the *ba* and *ka* fuse after a successful journey through the land of the dead, which may help explain some of the confusion over the number of parts of the soul. The justified dead are referred to as the *akhu*. For those who subscribe to reincarnation, one way to visualise this is as a tree. The eternal *akh* is the trunk of the tree, forever surging upwards. The personality of each incarnation is more like a branch being put out from the trunk. Each tree trunk could have numerous branches sprouting over the course of millennia.

7) The *Sah* is the spiritual body in which the *Khu* dwells for a period. *Sah* is the word for a mummy, the preserved and duly ritualised corpse which can be utilised for movement after death. A number of religions have believed in the resurrection of the corpse and the need to preserve the body in a condition fit for this – hence the strong objections to cremation by Christians until comparatively recently. The wish to preserve the *sah* may reflect the underlying belief that it would one day be needed again.

8) The *Sekhem* is the power or vital force in humans and elsewhere, which might be compared to the Chinese notion of chi or George Lucas' concept of the Force which permeates his fictional world and can be wielded by those trained in the art. *Sekhem* is the vital, creative force that holds things together ad flows forth in creative, expressive activities. Practical experience suggests that living beings (a category that is quite broad) have what could almost be called a signature to their *sekhem* – those sensitive to such things can pick up on not only a general trace of *sekhem* but identify the individual source of it. Pharaohs carried a *sekhem* sceptre to demonstrate their power and command. There is some indication that on state occasions the monarch would carry two, one for Setekh and one for Heru (respective patrons of Upper and Lower Egypt) and that each would be passed over an offering to indicate that it was accepted by each deity in turn. Since a metaphysical experience in 1980 Patrick Ziegler has applied the term to notions of reiki and spiritual healing, which has proved popular.

9) The *Ren*, which has been mentioned several times in earlier chapters, is the name of an individual, the very essence of who and what they are. There was a very real concern that, should one's name be forgotten after death (which, if we are realistic, almost everybody's name will be soon enough) then this will have a deleterious effect on the person's experience of the afterlife. The Egyptians shared the Shakespearian notion of name as reputation – *"he that filches from me my* good name *robs* me of that which not enriches him and makes me poor indeed". If being forgotten was doom, being thought unjustly ill of was little better. For the dead, their *ren* is their lasting reputation or legacy.

Jan Assmann (1998) reflects on the concern expressed by various Egyptian poets that disjuncture occurred between different parts of the gestalt individual occurred and led to problems which would get worse over time. One line from a poem about Memphis conjures up a vivid image that might strike a chord with many readers: *uresh-i iu ab-i nemau* (*I am awake but my heart is sleeping*). In the healthy, stable individual all these parts work in harmony, where *isfet* begins to creep in some parts either stop actively functioning (as per the sleeping *ab*) or begin to pull in conflicting directions. Mental, spiritual, and physical malaises can be understood as symptomatic of fractures within this dynamic notion of Self. Assmann uses the rather lovely imagery of a constellation to describe the way in which people function not as singular entities but as compositions of many different forces which contribute to their overall sense of identity. People invest themselves in relationships which define them as a parent, a sibling, a friend; careers define identities, as do hobbies and convictions such as politics or religion; certain possessions can simultaneously shape and express identity (houses and cars are obvious examples in the modern world).

Assmann highlights how the ancient person feared social isolation. Whilst it is popular to eschew such things today, it remains true. When relationships are lost to death or estrangement, part of identity goes with it. The more relationships that are lost, the greater the shattering of the Self. Some poor people see their entire families wiped out in singular events – house fires, car crashes, acts of war etc. – and the shock can destroy their sense of self and any capacity to rebuild their own lives. Many people in such situations often wonder if they even really have a life left once all their most important social relations are stripped away in a single, dreadful moment.

The way we understand our sense of Self is largely through the lens of relationships that build up over a lifetime and which stretch over a wide array of possibilities. Alongside the obvious friendship and family relationships, our links to pets are significant shapers of character as are the bonds between the farmer and their land, the teacher and pupil, employer and employee, artist and model.

Chapter Seven

The Netjeru

There are a vast number of Netjeru listed in historic sources, and it is not always evident if some of them are multiple titles for the same entities. For the sake of brevity, this chapter will explore five of the Netjeru for whom the author has a certain tendresse (useful sources for others can be found in the bibliography). Each entry includes some detail on festival dates related to the Netjer and for the sake of ease a brief overview of the calendar is given here – bearing in mind there is no singular Ancient Egyptian calendar but a number of them which developed and changed over time. Schott (1950) lays a version out as below drawing details from ritual calendars found in the temple list of Rameses III and also of Tutmose III. Von Beckerath (1980) gave rather precise dates for each of the 30-day *paen* or months (also noted on the table below) in keeping with the civic calendar (used for pragmatic issues of business, taxation, and the like) which fixed itself at dates that approximately coincided with the flooding and receding of the Nile. The religious calendar was more inclined to wait for the certain key events, such as the Flood, to actually happen before celebrating them.

Different Egyptologists have varying views as to the precise dates of the calendar when it comes to mapping it on to modern dates. Should the reader prefer a different system than the von Beckerath one used below, then they will need to work out the dates accordingly.

SEASON	EGYPTIAN NAME	COPTIC NAME	MODERN PERIOD
Akhet, the Flooding	*Tekh*	Thoth	August 29th to September 27th
	Menkhet	Panipet	September 28th to October 27th
	Het-Heru	Hathor	October 28th to November 26th
	Nehebkau	Khoiak	November 27th to December 26th
Peret, the Growing	*Shefbedet*	Tobi	December 27th to January 25th
	Rekehwer	Mekhir	January 26th to February 24th
	Rekehnedjes	Phamenoth	February 25th to March 26th
	Renenutet	Pharmouthi	March 27th to April 25th
Shemu, the Harvesting	*Khons*	Pakhon	April 26th to May 25th
	Khentkhety	Paoni	May 26th to June 24th
	Ipet-hemet	Ipip	June 25th to July 24th
	Wepet-renpet (also *Mesut-ra*)	Mesori	July 25th to August 23rd
The epagomenal days	*Hereyu-Renpet*		August 24th to August 28th

Seshet, Lady of the Library

Sphere of influence – writing, publishing, collecting, or understanding books; architecture, surveying, and building; astrology and astronomy; mathematics, preservation of political speeches.

Festival dates – the only date recorded is the Sed festival in the 30th year of a pharaoh's reign (a devotee might substitute the pharaoh with whoever the political leader of their own country happens to be, should they be unlucky enough to have one who drags on for three decades).

Other titles – Sefket-Abwy (She of seven points); Safekh-Abui (She who wears Two Horns); Nebet Per Medjat (Lady of the Library)

Suggested offerings – leaves of the persea tree; a scroll; writing utensils – especially those that are to be reserved for writing things of a sacred nature; the act of scribing itself, should the devotee write something in hieroglyphic or demotic as part of the ceremony; whilst not an offering per se, this author has found meditating on a heptagram arrangement of candles to be a conducive way of connecting.

Described as the consort, or sometimes daughter, of the ibis-headed Tehuti (whom the Greeks called Thoth) she shared the guardianship of scribes and writers with her husband. The ambiguity of the relationship is a common feature of many mythologies around the world where there are differing conceptions of how two entities are related. Atheist readings of the literature might regard this as evidence that these were all works of fictions and that assorted tribal communities each had their own spin on the tales. A more mystical interpretation might suggest that the Netjeru are far removed from human experience and notions of marriage, parenthood etc. are simply human attempts at describing something that really sits outside the range of our languages – so that, from one angle, the relationship between Seshet and Tehuti may seem like that between wife and husband, whilst from another stance more like father and daughter, yet in truth it is more complex than either.

Seshet guards the celestial *Per Ankh*, the Egyptian term for a library literally translating as the House of Life, and all earthly libraries. This heavenly *Per Ankh* might be regarded as the

Egyptian sense of what Helena Blavatsky and the Theosophists called the Akashic Records, an account of everything that has happened (at least the interesting parts!). Or it may have been more like a cross between the Library of Alexandria and the British Library, with a copy of everything ever written and strange creatures in the vaults. Seshet also watches over those who write the books that fill library shelves as well as those that maintain the Dewey-Decimal system. Like a divine version of Hypatia, she is also the goddess of mathematicians, accountants, astronomers, architects, and horologists ~ the latter because it is she who measures the passage of time. Rather like the Moirai of Greece, she also paced out the length of the pharaoh's reign.

She is depicted in human form, lacking the animal-head of most other deities, and normally wearing the leopard skin cloak of a funerary priestess. She records the names and deeds of the blessed dead, the *Akhu,* upon the leaves of the Tree of Life (usually thought to be a persea tree, *Mimusops Schimperi,* which was a popular addition to funerary bouquets and regarded as the tree which enveloped the washed-up coffin of Asur). This record of names and deeds may itself be the collection of the *Per Ankh.* It seems appropriate that the cosmic library should be an inscribed tree. One funeral text has her saying, *"My hand writes the length of his reign as it comes out from the mouth of Ra. My pen is Eternity, my ink is Forever."* One ancient text was called 'The Immortality of Writers' and praise the craft of scribing as the one guaranteed route to eternal life, or at any rate eternal memory in the minds of readers. It is easy to imagine Seshet approving of such a notion.

As a goddess of builders and architects, she was invoked at the start of any temple building project with a ritual known as *Pedjeshes* (Stretching the Cord). In this ceremony the Pharaoh would symbolically start the work by using a plumb line to take measurements ~ not unlike the habit of calling in modern day dignitaries to either lay the first brick, or dig the first shovel-full of soil. Should the reader wish to dedicate a room of their house or an area of their garden to the worship of the Netjeru, Seshet would be an appropriate goddess to call upon when starting the work of creating a permanent shrine.

In a world without mass literacy the invention of writing, which the Egyptians attributed to Seshet (though it was Tehuti who actually passed it on to humanity), enabled a tiny number of people to expand the potential of memory almost without limit. No longer did knowledge depend on the accuracy or extent of mortal memory. Writing enabled access to far more knowledge than could be contained in any one mind, and the containment provide by literacy stabilised knowledge – removing the vagaries of forgetfulness and blurred memory. The word hieroglyph comes from the Greek, meaning sacred writing. In the Egyptian tongue the pictograms were called *medu netjer*, words of the Gods. The spoken word was the basis of spoken magic, *heka*, and so Seshet may be considered a deity who made possible the *wedja* (amulet magic) so beloved of both ancient and modern pagans. The people of Kemet made extensive use of amulets and talismans at almost every point in life.

Was Seshet the entity who instructed humanity in the use of the written word, or is she a being that comes into existence through the very act of translating thought into squiggles on a page? Perhaps this either-or question is a false dichotomy and Seshet is both these things at once, and more besides. Writing conveys my thoughts over countless miles and hundreds or even thousands of years. My thoughts are now in your head, thanks to the medium of the sacred symbols! *Nebet Per Medjat* has granted a form of immortality through the sigils you are now reading, a gift to those who learn to write and read, or who are even just lucky enough be written about. As Seshet almost said, my laptop is Eternity and my ink-cartridge Forever.

Books and scrolls (and even eBooks, may the Netjeru help us) enable us to transcend time and space. They are bigger, on the inside, as the consort of Seshet almost said ~ one of Tjehuti's titles is Neb Nehes, Lord of Eternal Time, which answers a question best never asked. Terry Pratchett's conception of L-space seems to fit exceedingly well into the goddess's *Per Ankh*. Seshet's capacity to record is also her capacity to preserve the existence of those who write, and to enable those who read to contact the dead authors. When one considers the profoundly magical nature of writing, it becomes all the sadder to consider what utter crap most people who put pen to paper, or finger to cell phone, produce!

The hieroglyphic symbol of Seshet has posed something of a puzzle. Seen on the top of her head, a long vertical line leads to a circle from which radiate seven shorter lines or petal-like shapes ~ all of this contained under the umbrella of what looks like upturned horns. Egyptologists have yet to decipher the meaning, though some have suggested it may be a papyrus plant, largely due to its use in the creation of Egyptian libraries. However, the symbol for papyrus is already known, which suggests this means something else. One alternate theory is that the botanical design is actually either a lotus flower or a stylised cannabis leaf, this latter plant being used by the Egyptians both as a recreational drug, as a medicine, and for making various hemp products.

Musing on the image inspires me with various thoughts, such as how the arched horns put me in mind of the goddess Nut, embodiment of the sky, who stretches over the prone form of her brother-lover Qeb, lord of the earth. The *Pedjeshes* ceremony was conducted at night, so the temple could be aligned with the stars. One account talks of the ceremony tying the building to Ursa Major, whose seven brightest stars form the Plough. The radiating lines may represent the stars of the Plough constellation. The longer line may possibly be the stretched-out cord used by the pharaoh.

Seshet seems to appreciate the celebration and creation of literature as part of rituals to honour her. The imagery of lives inscribed on leaves of the Tree of Life might also serve to inspire a central act in ritual, a good way of honouring the dead or those who create and contribute towards libraries. It could also be a meditative focus for participants in a ceremony to reflect on what of their own lives (to date) might be written on leaves of the Tree. The name written should, of course, be the *ren* or sacred name and communing with Seshet may be a way of establishing what the name of one's core is. The persea tree is part of the laurel family, so other laurels could be used as a substitute if the Egyptian plant proves difficult to find in your neighbourhood. Avocadoes are part of the same genus, and might be offered as a food in ritual as an acceptable alternative to the Egyptian fruit.

Setekh, Lord of the Desert

Sphere of influence – the desert and its dangerous creatures; ruthlessness; foreigner visitors and immigrants; storms; beer making and brewing in general

Festival dates – Battle of Setekh and Heru (26th day of Tekh, which by von Beckerath's civic calendar is 23rd September) followed by the Day of Peace; the Judgement of Re on the Dispute (23rd day of Het-Heru, which equates to 19th November); Going Forth of Setekh (17th day of Renenutet, or 12th April); Birthday of Setekh (third of the epagomenal days, 26th August on the civic calendar)

Other titles – Neb Qeri (Lord of the Storm); Nubti (He of the Golden City of Nubt); Deser Fa'a (Red Haired One); Seker Apepi (He Who Overthrows Apepi); Imy Senket (He Who is in the Darkness)

Suggested offerings – the *was* sceptre; lettuce; melon; beer; gold; images of hippopotamuses, crocodiles, scorpions, *nehes* (the mysterious set-beast), wild pigs, or donkeys

The red-haired brother of Asur looms large in Egyptian mythology, and poses a challenge for any Kemetic as they come to terms with him. Over the years a number of writers have viewed Setekh as a prototype for Satan, with all the baggage that such a description comes with. The hair colour is a direct tie to the ochre red land of *deshret*, the root of our modern word desert. That shade also holds significance for the Netjeret Sekhmet who drinks the ochre-dyed beer that lulls her to sleep after destroying all the wicked humans on Earth. Come the dawn light, lion-headed Sekhmet has transformed into the cow-headed Het-Heru who spreads love and attraction in the world.

The exact meaning of his name is debated, by scholars of the day such as Plutarch have suggested it may be something like "overpowering" or "overwhelming". Murray suggests it may allude to drunkenness and translate as something like "He who makes people drunk", and he is a deity much associated with beer and the wildness that descends on many people after they have had a few too many.

In section 23 of the Papyrus of Ani there is reference to Setekh being the deity who places fetters around the mouth of the dead, which are subsequently loosened with the correct magical formula. Whilst this might be interpreted in a villainous light, it could also be seen as a natural and necessary function of a deity connected to the dead. Just as the newly dead in Greek religion drank from the waters of the River Lethe and lost their memories (perhaps a blessed relief in many cases, and explanatory of why so few people remember much of anything about past lives) so the silencing of the dead for Egyptians might have been a required step. Obviously, a corpse cannot speak, but the grieving commonly feels the absence of their relative or friend in a more metaphysical sense – that the person is not around in a spiritual way, cannot be felt nor respond to tearful communiques. The ceremony for Opening the Mouth was primarily intended to grant the deceased voice again, the power not only to chatter with their fellow dead but also to the living. More importantly it granted the capacity to use *heka*, magical speech, with which to have potent influence for the greater good. The initial process of dying, from the Kemetic view, was to lose that ability, to cease to have any say in the community of beings. Setekh it was who shut the mouth of the newly dead, requiring them to rely on mourners with the know-how to give them back the power of speech. Those who died uncared for were doomed to remain speechless.

As a god who seeks to violate his nephew in order to gain the throne, he forces 21st century devotees to look at a practice which most would now regard as anathema. The act reflects an era in which someone attaining to a position of power had to be seen not only as strong but unsullied. These days many, probably most, people would have sympathy for the victim of an abusive act and perceive their capacity to survive as a great strength. Many might regard the ancient Kemetic approach as victim-shaming, which to a large extent it was.

The ruthlessness which Setekh demonstrates here is, in some respects, reminiscent of the similar ferocious determination which Odin exhibits in many Norse tales where he will do whatever it takes to attain a goal, no matter the cost to himself or others. It is the kind of quality openly admired in leaders of the ancient Mediterranean cultures, and still admired in countless places around the world today – from the boardroom to the war room to the state room. It is a ferociously dangerous trait, responsible for endless tragedy in the world, but equally as responsible for survival against all odds. In the divisive identity politics of the early 21st century it is likely to be labelled as "toxic masculinity", but it is the same steely-eyed fury to be found in the mother cat that eviscerates anyone foolish enough to threaten her kittens.

For all the rather devilish imagery that congregates around him, it must be remembered that Setekh stands at the prow of the sun barque every night as it descends in Duat. It is he that fights off the countless monsters and fiends that besiege the sun god on his journey through the wee small hours. It is he who battles the very embodiment of mayhem and collapse itself, the vast serpent Apepi. This is where his wild ruthlessness comes into its own; doing what must be done to protect those he serves and loves. To paraphrase an old friend, Setekh is the kind of Netjer that a person is best advised to have as an ally rather than an enemy.

Setekh is assisted by a legion of beings called the *mesu badesh*, which Budge (1895) interpreted with suitable Victorian zeal as demons in the biblical sense. Some modern-day diabolists have also run with this view, calling upon the Children of Rebellion. They are the 72 followers who aid in sealing Asur into the sarcophagus, and keeping all possible assistance at bay whilst the revolution takes place.

The creatures associated with the Red Lord are mostly deadly ones. The hippopotamus is his, a beast that kills more humans than any other mammal in Africa. It was in the form of this river behemoth that he fought one of his many battles with Heru. He also has the wild pig, crocodile, and the much less deadly antelope and donkey. Pork was not a popular dish in Egypt (as with most very hot countries prior to the development of refrigeration, it goes rancid too quickly to be safe to eat), but pigs were reared to provide lard which was used in cosmetics, medications, as oil for lamps, and similar uses. The Tale of Heru and the Pig gives a more mystical explanation, that during one of their many fights Setekh injured one of his nephew's eye which swelled up and resembled a black pig. The sight of his bruise caused Heru to feint and Re declared that the pig was an abomination to Heru, drawing the antipathy of the other gods towards that animal in sympathy for the wounded Netjer. Despite liking a bacon sandwich as much as the next omnivore, this author would not offer pork to Setekh but would use porcine iconography on the altar. The prime animal associated with this Netjer, the *nehes*, remains an unidentified mystery – assorted Egyptologists have speculated as to what the square-eared, fork-tailed creature might be: greyhound, anteater, or perhaps an entirely imaginary one. Setekh is commonly given as the father of lupine Wepwawet and of jackal-headed Anpu, which might suggest that his own animal head is a member of the canine family (whether a regular animal or a fantastical one). There is a curious echo here between the character of Setekh and that of the Norse Loki, who is also the father of a great wolf.

He is the unrelenting heat of the desert and the ever-present threat of drought and the death that goes with it. Somewhat contradictorily he is also connected to storms, both giving and taking desperately needed rain water.

Spell 42 of the *Ru Nu Peret Em Heru* equips the newly deceased with a verse to recite in their defence in which different body parts are associated with different deities. It is unlikely to be a random list, but rather these sections of the anatomy have some symbolic association with each of the deities in question. As can be seen below the Red Lord is associated with the back, possibly because he stands at the very front of the barque seeking the enemies of Re and so the passengers and crew always see the rear view of him. The phallus of Asur obviously indicates the spell was to be said by a man – presumably a different deity being called upon if the soul were a woman.

My hair is Nu; my face is Re; my eyes are Het-Heru; my ears are Wepwawet; my nose is She who presides over her lotus leaf; my lips are Anpu; my molars are Selkis; my incisors are Aset the goddess; my arms are the Ram, the Lord of Mendes; my breast is Neith, Lady of Sais; my back is Setekh; my phallus is Asur; my muscles are the Lords of Kheraha; my chest is he who is greatly majestic; my belly and my spine are Sekhmet; my buttocks are the Eye of Heru; my thighs and my calves are Nut; my feet are Ptah; my toes are living falcons; there is no member of mine devoid of a god, and Tehuti is the protection of all my flesh.

Wepwawet, Opener of the Ways

Sphere of influence – victory in battle; military strategy; defence and rejuvenation of the monarch; justice; hunting (especially with bow and arrows); opening the gateways between life and death; protector of the dead

Festival dates – Sed festival

Other titles – Sed (One with a Tail); Neb ta Deser (Lord of the Sacred Land, a metaphor for the graveyards)

Suggested offerings – keys; *hedj* mace; bow and arrows; images of wolves; fur or teeth from a wolf

A dispute exists as to whether the grey animal depicted as Wepwawet's head is a wolf, as the Greeks believed (and so translated the name of his chief site of worship as Lycopolis, City of the Wolf) or a jackal. The *canis anthus lupaster* has been defined as both a wolf and a jackal by different zoologists. Personal gnosis suggests Wepwawet is decidedly lupine in nature, but other people will equally swear that their gnosis reveals him to be a jackal. Perhaps, like most divine beings, he is whatever he wishes to be on a given occasion.

A probable son of Setekh, though the exact family tree is variable depending on the sources read, he stands as the brother to Anpu (Anubis) and shares a dual function with him in their service to both the souls and bodies of the dead.

His name may be translated as either Opener of the Ways or Opener of the Roads. In this latter capacity it is possible that he may have had patronage over travellers and those who create roadways. Other titles attributed to him include Extinguisher of Breaths, a role suggestive of the Death itself and perhaps a being that not only severs the final ties of life but maybe guides the soul on the journey into the afterlife.

Wepwawet is a key figure in the ceremony of the Opening of the Mouth, which was once performed over mummified bodies as a means to grant them speech and other capacities in the afterlife.

The only known part of the festival calendar associated with the wolf god is the Heb-Sed, which is not so much yearly as a jubilee to mark the thirtieth anniversary of a pharaoh's reign and again at three to four year intervals consequent to that (very few rulers living long enough to mark many of those). For a 21st century devotee the Sed festival would be rare to impossible, depending on the country a person lived in. Whilst a British monarch could potentially see out three decades on the throne (the current one at the time of writing certainly has), an American president fortunately cannot be so long in office. The festival, if it is to be marked at all, would need to be adapted to celebrate the idea of long service by whatever stretch of time that is understood in the devotee's homeland. If the Heb-Sed is to be regarded as a celebration of long rule by the national leader (in whichever country the person is resident) then it raises a philosophical question as to whether all leaders should be equally honoured or if the individual Kemetic should exercise some personal political bias in only honouring the reign of rulers of whom they approve. In a ritual group this could lead to a potential degree of tension, should some members admire and wish to honour a politician or monarch whom other members despise. Whilst attendance at religious ritual must always be voluntary, it clearly becomes somewhat awkward if there are members staying away effectively as a protest rather than due to some pragmatic concern (childcare difficulties, or such like). The activities of the Heb-Sed required the pharaoh to engage in various activities which could hardly be expected of a modern political leader, so a deal of adaptation would be needed.

In Spell 42 of the *Ru Nu Peret Em Heru*, given earlier in this chapter, Wepwawet is associated with the ears which may be suggestive of the alert wolf of the desert always keeping an ear open for sounds of prey or of potential threat. The list of body parts could also be seen as indicative of which deity to turn to for healing with respect to illnesses or injuries to that region.

Those wishing to commune with the wolf god in ritual are welcome to use the following poem of the author's own devising. It has previously featured in the collect 'Moon Poets' by the same publisher.

Awaken in peace
Beloved of the sun
Awaken in peace
Follower of the moon.

Desert wanderer,
Maker of tracks
In the pathless wastes,
Grey light in a red land.

The door is bolted to me,
Confined within my mind,
Opener of the ways,
Unlock what I cannot.

Let me ride besides you
In the barque of Re,
Worlds open before us.
Danger abounds, my soul yearns!

Howling in the darkness,
I shiver to your hot breath.
Let me be open, let me be open
And live, let me not sleep.

Sobek

Sphere of influence – victory in battle; the military; justice

Festival dates – birthday on the 11th day of the month of Rekehwer (5th February); removal of the deity's tongue on 14th day of the month of Khons (9th May... though whether this date was celebrated by his devotees or only by those of whichever deity did the slicing is now unclear); on the 4th day of Nehebkau (30th November) festivals of an unspecified nature were held for the crocodile god

Other titles – Neb Hep (Lord of the Creeks); Neb Hapi (Lord of the Nile); Neb Hat (Lord of Strife); Neb Entyu (Lord of Myrrh)

Suggested offerings – images of crocodiles; myrrh; juniper berries (suitable for incense when dried)

The name Sobek may mean "he who reassembles" echoing to a very early myth in which he assisted Aset with putting her brother-husband's corpse back together. With the conflicting accounts of family dynamics in Egyptian mythology, Sobek may be the son of Setekh and Neith. His worship was centred on Shedyet, which the Greeks called Crocodopolis. One tradition has it that Sobek's sweat is the source of the Nile. One of the festivities associated with him is the cutting out of his tongue, in retribution for his involvement with the death of Asur. The details of this link are now lost, but he is also described as protecting the child Heru during the period when he and his mother are hiding from Setekh.

One of the Coffin Texts, Spell 991, refers to a story whose details are now unclear (or yet to be translated) where Sobek is referred to as having his tongue "cut out because of the mutilation of Asur". Some sources mention a version of the Great

Royal Myth in which it is Sobek rather than the oxyrhynchus fish that consumes the dead god's phallus, so this may be a reference to that spin on the story. The Maxims of Amememope contain reference to a crocodile deprived of his tongue, stating that fear of him is negligible. The verse is a general warning not to blab information or generally speak foolishly. The tongueless crocodile may be a metaphor for a previously powerful being whose might has been lost along with its capacity for wise speech.

Many mythologies include stories where a character who is initially hostile to the hero or heroine later becomes an ally to the cause, and perhaps Sobek may have been perceived in this light in a tale now missing. In Spell 32 of the *Ru Nu Peret Em Heru* the deceased is meant to recite the following verse to repel eight crocodiles that attack it on the journey through the afterlife:

> *Get back you crocodile of the West, who lives on the Unwearying Stars!*
> *Detestation of you is in my belly, for I have absorbed the power of Asur, and I am Setekh.*
> *Get back, you crocodile of the West! The nau-snake is in my belly, and I have not given myself to you, your flame will not be on me.*

The nau-snake is a mythical entity rather than a species of earthly serpent. Jeremy Nadler (2004) identifies it with the serpentine Nehebkau, guardian of Duat, as a dispenser and potential remover of the *ka*. The identity of these crocodiles is not established, but they may be agents of a hostile aspect of Sobek who (giving a more positive spin) seeks to test the mettle of the journeying *mut* spirit.

Some regions regarded Sobek as the consort of the snake goddess Renenutet, one of whose functions was to give out or reveal the sacred names, the *ren*. She was also the mother of the aforementioned Nehebkau, though the father was commonly seen as Qeb rather than the great crocodile.

Sobek is also referred to as having recourse to robbery, which might link to his military patronage where victorious armies would help themselves to the spoils of war. Many people in these more liberal days tend to shy away from the brutal nature of warfare, and might find plundering a distasteful idea or wring their hands in guilt for ancestral wrongs. Our distant ancestors, and many still around the world today, are not so averse. The chances of modern Kemetic devotees to the crocodile god being directly involved in warfare and being in the position to claim trophies of battle are fairly low. However, not all battles are fought by soldiers – there are other types of conflict and people might find themselves able to claim the spoils of triumphs in boardroom fights, spats between rival sports teams, or even warfare between criminal gangs.

Applying the four forms of medieval hermeneutics to the story of the tongue cutting, it may be seen as:

1) exactly what it appears to be, the silencing of the crocodile god
2) an allegorical account of something – perhaps removing the voice or influence of the military from the politics of the royal court in retaliation for some attack on a long dead pharaoh
3) a more anagogical or metaphysical understanding might be that the forceful lusts and rages that the crocodile embodies become silenced through spiritual awakening
4) the moralist message that speaking with the voice of anger or coarse desire might undermine both oneself and society at large

Herodotus, not always the most reliable of sources, suggests that attitudes to crocodiles (and perhaps by extension to other species as well) were variable in different regions of Kemet.

The Thebans adored them and considered them divine to the extent of keeping the as pets and giving them jewelled collars and the like to wear, whilst the people of Elephantine ate them. It is not unreasonable to suppose that the sacred totems of one place might be the annoying pests or main courses of another, and that the wish to see a consistent culture is a product of modern minds looking back rather than a lived reality of the day. The practicality of raising a baby crocodile as a pet and taking an adult one for walkies is not something with which this author is familiar, but perhaps some readers might be in a position to suggest whether Herodotus' claim is a realistic one or something born of misunderstanding or hyperbole. In this era the dangerous pets' trade is a terribly destructive one and it cannot be recommended that any modern Kemetic try rearing a sacred crocodile at home. Those wishing to devote themselves to the children of Sobek are encouraged to support them in the wild through suitable charities or maybe provide aid to local zoos, safari parks and the like many of which have sponsorship schemes.

With regard to rituals centred around Sobek, chapter 88 of the Book of the Dead contains a spell by which the newly deceased can take the form of Sobek. This may have been something retained for the discarnate soul rather than the living, but could be used as part of a ritual to experience the presence of the crocodile within ones very being.

Inek Sobek Hor-ib neru'ef, inek sobek it em awa
Inek remy wer a'a em kem-wer
Inek neb kesu em khem
I am Sobek amid his dread, I am Sobek who seizes by violence
I am the grand sea-creature, great in Kemwer
I am the lord of reverence in Khem

Het-Heru

Sphere of influence – love, passion, desire, sexuality, peace, forgiveness, cattle, beauty, cosmetics (making, applying, and wearing them), beauticians

Festival dates – on the 20th day of the month of Tekh (17th September) a festival of drunkenness to celebrate the shift from Sekhmet to Hert-heru was held; the goddess Aset received the horns of Het-Heru on the 26th day of the same month (23rd September, which is commonly the autumn equinox), perhaps indicating a transfer of power; on the 1st day of the following month of Het-Heru, named after the goddess (28th October), a great feast was held in her honour; the birthday of the goddess was celebrated on the 12th day of Menkhet (9th October); a day for the joint celebration of Het-Heru and Sekhmet was held on the 13th of Shefbedet (8th January); a shared festival with the cat-headed goddess Bast takes place on the first day of Ipet-hemet (25th June, or one might opt for the summer solstice), and another four days later marking her return to the land of Punt, much to the regret of the other deities

Other titles – Nebet Nub (Lady of Gold); Neb Mefkhat (Lady of Turquoise); Neb Shesmet (Lady of Malachite); Nebet Akhakh (Lady of the Stars, or more poetically Lady of the Flowers of the Sky); Nebet Khebi (Lady of the Dance, although this could also be interpreted as Lady of the Acrobatics)

Suggested offerings – sistrum; images of cows; milk; myrrh, leaves and wooden items etc. from the sycamore tree (powdered bark can be used as incense too); turquoise (both the precious stone and objects that are of this colour), lapis lazuli, and malachite; gold; dancing – especially sensuous dance or athletic, vigorous dance; hand mirrors

One tale recounts how the lion goddess Sekhmet emerged into the world as the manifestation of divine rage, when Re grew tired of the endless complaining of humanity. The lion stalked the earth devouring the wicked, but developed such a taste for human flesh that her definition of "wicked" grew broader and broader until there were so few people left that they pleaded for mercy from the Heavens. Re relented and instructed his devotees to dig a great pit and fill it with red ochre beer. The lioness saw the red lake and lapped it up, thinking it to be blood, before passing out drunk. In this unconscious state she transformed into the cow-headed Het-Heru, moving from a deity of wrath and vengeance to one of love and tenderness.

The goddess is associated with a number of precious stones including malachite, which was popularly ground down not only to make cosmetics but also for use in statue manufacture, decorating wall stelae and the like. One of the words for this stone, *wadj*, is also the general word for the colour green. At a semiotic level this colour not only represents the world of plants and links to associated skills (agriculture, herbalism and so on) but also to the spiritual theme of resurrection for the green-skinned Asur. Plants appear to die when harvested or during the sweltering season (in other parts of the world it is obviously the cold season that brings death) only to spring magically back to life. Het-Heru partakes of this restorative quality, and it is worth considering that the swirling patterns innate to a chunk of malachite might serve as a sort of naturally occurring mandala to meditate upon and loose oneself in for a consciousness shifting ritual.

In Spell 42 of the *Ru Nu Peret Em Heru*, given earlier in this chapter, Het-Heru is associated with the eyes, which seems suitable for a goddess of beauty, which is taken in through the eyes. As per the suggestion made earlier, it may also be appropriate to turn to her for aid with diseases or and injuries to the eyes.

In texts from late periods she was sometimes referred to as the Seven Het-Heru, which may be understood as seven messengers, like the *uputju* who will be briefly discussed in the next chapter, or as seven aspects of the one Netjeret acting as a gestalt entity. The seven feature mainly in places and literary sources from the Graeco-Roman period and it could be that these beings reflect ideas more rooted to those cultures than native to Egypt itself. In the Tale of the Two Brothers and also in the Tale of the Doomed Prince the heptad appear over the cradle to deliver prophecies, which Sandra Ottens (2012) likens to the seven fairy godmothers who appear in the pre-Disney version of Sleeping Beauty and arguably represent the seven astronomical forces then popularly used to draw up horoscopes. In a similar vein, the seven Het-Heru women may be representative of astrological influences which ay out the destiny of the new born. One of their tasks in the stories mentioned is to predict how the child just born will eventually die. To some extent this could be seen as similar to the Greek Fates measuring out the length of a life.

Much like the handmaidens who attend the Norse goddess Frig, each of the seven has their own qualities and may be honoured individually or as a collective. The Names of the Seven Het-Heru, at least when they are in bovine form, are found inscribed in the tomb of Nefertari. Translations of their names vary, but suggested ones are given here:

Het Kau Nebet Tcher – Lady on the limits of the dwelling of souls
Sentet Utheset – The Silent One
Amentit Khentet Auset –The One from the West
Hatet Sahet – The Lady from the North
Urt Meru Tesert – The Beloved with Red Hair
Khenemet Ankhet – Consort of Life
Sekhem Ren-es em Abet-es – Her Name Prevails

However the reader conceives of the Seven, they could be turned to at the birth of a child to grant their blessings, or communicated with during an act of divination to prognosticate something useful about the life ahead of the new born. Where the parents of the child appreciate Egyptian art, a painted papyrus or figurines representing the Seven might be a nice addition to the child's bedroom to watch over their infancy.

One love charm translated by Borghouts (1978) by which a man might win the love of the woman he desires invokes the Seven, describing them as robed in red linen. This visual image might influence any artwork the reader creates or purchases, as well as how the goddesses are envisioned. This particular spell is a rather odd one in that it incorporates a threat to burn down Busiris if the goddesses fail to deliver. Whilst this may have been an accepted outlook of the original writer of the spell, it is hardly an attitude to be encouraged today!

A rather beautiful hymn to the Seven is found in a crypt at the Temple of Het-Heru at Dendera, translated into German by Junker von Hermann (1906) and thence to English. It is included here so that the reader may both enjoy it and consider its use in ritual or a prayer. The verse lends itself to being spoken whilst the *ser* (a type of tambourine) is played.

HYMN TO THE SEVEN HATHORS
We play the ser for Your Ka,
We dance for Your Majesty,
We exalt You
To the height of Heaven.
You are the Lady of Sekhem,
The Menat and the Sistrum,
The Lady of Music,
For whose Ka one plays.

We praise Your Majesty every day,
From dusk until the earth grows light,

We rejoice in Your Countenance, O Lady in Dendera!
We praise You with song.
You are the Lady of Jubilation, the Lady of the Iba-dance,
The Lady of Music, the Lady of Harp-playing,
The Lady of Dancing, the Lady of Tying on Garlands,
The Lady of Myrrh, and the Lady of Leaping.

We glorify Your Majesty,
We give praise before Your Face.
We exalt Your Power
Over the Gods and the Goddesses.
You are the Lady of Hymns,
The Lady of the Library,
The Great Seshat
At the head of the Mansion of Records.

We propitiate Your Majesty every day.
Your heart rejoices at hearing our songs.
We rejoice when we see You, day by day.
Our hearts are jubilant when we see Your Majesty.
You are the Lady of Garlands, the Lady of Dance,
The Lady of Unending Drunkenness.
We rejoice before Your face; we play for Your Ka.
Your heart rejoices over our performance

Chapter Eight

Other Spirit Beings

As with pretty much all cultures, the number of entities less powerful than the deities proliferates and much lore may have been lost over the millennia. The dead have been mentioned a number of times already, but take such a central part in the Kemetic view of reality that they must be considered again.

Broadly speaking the dead come under two categories, appearing as either *Akh* or *Mut* – Transfigured or Unblessed. The *akhu* are those who, through a combination of saintly lives and proper funeral rites, have attained a holy status in the world beyond and are able to assist the living. The *mutu* are somewhat ambiguous in that the word can refer to the dead in a broadly generic way as those on their journey to the Afterlife but without yet having attained transfiguration, but also those who have specifically failed to get there and so exist in a tormented state – what most Europeans would probably think of as ghosts. The rather blissful view of the Afterlife outlined in previous chapters is reflective of early Egyptian views. Later on, such as in the Middle Kingdom, opinions began to shift somewhat and an increasing number of people saw the next world as mostly spent loitering around one's tomb. This could be pleasant if the tomb were well-kept and had plenty offerings left in it, but for the forgotten or deliberately neglected, the prospect was grey and monotonous (rather like the view a lot of Greeks had as to what lay in store for those who failed to make it through to the Elysian Fields).

The *mutu* that become restless, tormented ghosts do so as the result of a number of possible factors including the lack of proper funeral rites offered them by the living, the traumatic nature of their death (murder, suicide etc.), and simply being generally horrible people in life who remain just as unpleasant after death. Where the lack of respectful rites is the problem, then the *mut* can be laid to rest by the provision of such. There are tales of haunted houses where murder victims seek help to get their secretly disposed corpses found and dealt with in a more respectable manner.

In Canaanite mythology the god of death is the insatiable and destructive Mot about who an incomplete tale survives detailing his conflict with Ba'al. His attempt to kill that deity results in the goddess Anat destroying him in a highly elaborate, ritualistic manner. Though turned to dust, Mot eventually resurrects after seven years to resume his vendetta. The feud is only finally resolved when the goddess Shapash shames Mot with the warning that he will alienate his own father through his rapacious desire to devour Ba'al and anyone who gets in his way. There is a certain similarity of temperament with the Egyptian understanding of the *mutu* and this Canaanite deity, in as much as both torment others and are seemingly insatiable in their hunger for offerings. A difference perhaps emerges in that the unhappy dead will accept voluntary offerings in preference to seizing morsels.

As medical texts indicate, the *mutu* were believed to cause illness in the living. As a notion, the idea of supernatural causations to illness is still adhered to in many cultures. If the reader is not from one of these cultures then they may wish to pause and reflect on how they understand the concept. It could simply be put in the box of quaint and curious things that people used to believe in a long time ago and forgotten about. Or it could be taken literally that the restless souls of unhappy dead people do indeed inflict suffering on the living. Alternately it may be regarded more as a metaphor. Many, if not most, Muslims believe that the jinn (a separate race of beings, rather than discarnate human souls) cause mental and bodily illness, though some theologians such as Mirza Tahir Ahmad risk the wrath of Salafi literalists by suggesting that jinn are poetic representations of viruses and germs, born from an era when modern scientific terminology and conceptualisation was unavailable. The Egypt of thousands of years ago also lacked this language, so could have used the imagery of invisible malign forces spreading disease to account for what we would now place in a Petrie dish. Ought the modern Kemeticist be performing rituals to placate the restless *mutu* or simply use bacterial hand-wash on a regular basis – or do both? We might additionally reflect that many diseases have a genetic component such that our ancestors do sometimes inflict illness upon us, though we are as likely to inherit such patterns from the shining dead as the tormented dead. There is some suggestion that these disconsolate souls inhabit a sort of inverted world wherein things that are considered beneficial for the living become harmful to them and vice versa. To some extent this seems to continue the notion that existence is much the same for those who wallow in *isfet*, whereby they take pleasure in things inimical to the well-adjusted and disdain what others take joy in. As Shakespeare said in King Lear, "Wisdom and goodness to the vile seem vile; Filths savour but themselves". A near identical sentiment is expressed by Ptahhotep in his collection of maxims where he rebukes disobedient sons who do not value virtue. Without wishing to seem too preachy, people are advised to consider not only the diets they feed to their bodies but also what they find wholesome mental fare.

The *mesu badesh* (also sometimes referred to as the *mesu Setekh*) have already been mentioned briefly in the previous chapter as the Children of Rebellion that serve Setekh. Very little detail is given about them in the translated texts, and whilst they are seen by Budge as essentially demonic powers it is unclear to what extent this is informed not only by Budge's own cultural background but also by the negativity heaped upon Setekh and anything connected to him as a result of the Hyksos occupation. It is uncertain if the *mesu* were always seen as malign beings, or if this was a gradual political erosion from a previously positive perception. Unsubstantiated personal gnosis suggests that Setekh himself may be a ruthless force linked to dangerous places and creatures, but he is not some Hammer Horror film monster. It may be that the *mesu* were considered a separate race in their own right, maybe somewhat akin to the djinn of Arabic lore and sired by the supposedly sterile Setekh, or that they once humans – priests and priestesses of Setekh who continued to serve the Red Lord after death in a special capacity and are his children in a more figurative sense. The significance of the 72 followers who assist in the attack on Asur is open to debate. It is a number that has several occurrences in the Bible, such as when Jesus sends out 72 followers to spread the word. This may be sheer coincidence, or the Jews may have picked up on the numerical symbolism and passed this on to the early Church. The Biblical reference is likely the source of the 72 followers who accompany the mythical Irish sage Fénius Farsaid when he sets out to gather the best of all languages in the world from which they then produce Gaelic as the most superior of all tongues. For a story committed to manuscript by monks, it is a bold assertion to suggest Irish is better even than the Latin of the Church or the Aramaic of Jesus!

The Lesser Key of Solomon, a book of magic compiled in the mid-1600s, details the 72 demons which King Solomon purportedly locked away with thaumaturgy. There is a huge gap of time between the Lesser Key and both the original compilation of Egyptian stories beforehand and their eventual translation afterwards with the Rosetta Stone discovery. No link can realistically be drawn, but it is an interesting echo and maybe the tradition of a band of malign beings sustained over time, transmitted from teacher to student in esoteric circles, even if nobody could recall how it started. In one of the myths ibis-headed Tehuti wins of a year from the intoxicated moon god Iabet whilst gambling with him. Through this means he gains the five days that become the epagomenal days on which the deities Asur, Aset, Heru the Elder, Setekh, and Neheb-het are born. It is possible there is some semiotic link between this fraction of time and the number of *mesu badesh*, but it is not a clear one – a topic for meditation perhaps. There is also the possibility that the *mesu* may have been inspired by the hated Hyksos and that the number 72 was connected to them. For example, it may have been the number of aristocratic leaders heading the invasion force and toppling the Egyptian-born pharaoh, symbolically killing Asur.

The period between death and transfiguration has similarities to the Catholic notion of Purgatory, during which the living are encouraged to pray on behalf of the dead and seek intercessions for them to help in their attainment of Heaven. Modern Kemetics need to consider the issue of death rituals in present times. The sorts of ceremonies required for the dead in the distant past can no longer be conducted (in many countries some aspects of those rituals are now illegal). Is it reasonable to suppose that all those devotees of the Netjeru who did not receive the full rites over the last 1800 or so years will have been wafting listless and malcontent in the spirit world? A more liberal view (though merely because this view is more upbeat does not in any way make it correct) might suggest that the critical factor in funerals is that they are conducted with good intent by the mourners rather than the efficacy being down to the exacting detail. The restless *mut* is maybe one who knows they are unmourned as does the ghost of Nebusemekh who plagues the living until finally Khonsemhab agrees to rebuild his dilapidated tomb, or who lacks the connection to their living family that a grave and due ceremony would provide. The answer which the reader comes to upon this issue must surely have some impact on the nature of their own funeral arrangements when the time comes.

The creature Ammut or Ammemet looms over the Afterlife as the force which consumes those hearts found to be too heavy with *isfet* to make it through to the Fields of A'alu. This strange being has the hind parts of a hippo, the foreparts on a lion, and the head of a crocodile. The heart devoured may simply cease to exist, a soul blinking out. It might be interpreted that whilst the *kha*, the divine spark, continues on into other forms, the loss of the ab represents the universe erasing all memory of the individual life that once was. If that *kha* reincarnates into a fresh body it does so without any recollection of the life eaten by Ammut. The imagery of the tripartite body may be simply an allusion to three very dangerous animals, or it may indicate that Ammut partakes of qualities of Sobek, Sekhmet, and Tuaret.

Apepi is a divine figure, but not necessarily one likely to inspire many people to acts of worship. He is the Great Serpent who embodies the force of *isfet*, seeking to defeat Re on his nightly journey through *Duat* and shatter the cosmos. Records indicate that his birthday was marked on the 22nd day of the month of Rekehnedjes (15th March), but there are no indications if this was a day of celebration, mourning, or something else again. It may have been seen as a very dark day on which to castigate the very existence of Apepi, perhaps by burning effigies of him. Or maybe a day on which he was supremely powerful and all people had to watch their step for fear of his destructive might. Just as there are people today who worship pain and discord, so they may have been people doing so in ancient times. There are also people who cannot resist a bad boy and always want to recast a villain in a more sympathetic role, so perhaps some distant Egyptians as well as some modern people saw the Great Serpent as a misunderstood proto-James Dean railing against the fossilised rule of Re.

Rita Lucarelli (2010) outlines various types of often dangerous beings that might be encountered. She broadly divides them into *shamayu*, wandering spirits, and *weretu*, who are guardians of specific places and are not expected to journey beyond their locales. One of the spells translated by Borghouts (1978) treats these beings, along with the *nedjesti* (whose name means the Incendiaries) and the *kha'yti* (Murderers), as particularly associated with Sekhmet. The correct performance of the spell is meant to keep the magician safe from plagues for a year, suggestive that (at least for those connected with the lion goddess) they were akin to the Greek *nosoi*, the disease spirits that escaped from Pandora's jar. In the context of illness perhaps the incendiary *nedjesti* could be spirits (or simply germs) that cause fever, burning up the body rather than burning down buildings. Sekhmet was regarded as both sending diseases to those who displeased her and curing the illnesses of those she favoured. Whilst the *weretu* seldom cause problems except in defence of their sacred place, the *shamayu* are more morally ambiguous and have to be treated with greater wariness. Somewhat like Old Testament angels, they are commonly messengers of deities but this does not mean that any sensible person should wish to encounter one in a dark alleyway. The *uputayu* are messengers of the deities, whilst the *hatayu* (which means slaughterers) may well act as divinely appointed assassins executing those who have offended the Netjeru. Artistic representations of these beings in wall friezes, papyri and so forth shows them as strange hybrid creatures composed of various different types of animals.

Chapter Nine

Applying the Concepts

The text so far has set out not only to present information that will aid the experienced and potential Kemeticist alike, but also pose questions for the reader to reflect upon and help inform their own practice. The nature of that practice will vary according to a great many factors which themselves will change and fluctuate over time – health, employment, family commitments, accommodation, spiritual experiences, and so forth. Whether the practice is solo, with intimate family members, or a wider circles of friends and associates will influence the nature of the spiritual discipline.

Where it is possible a daily practice is very beneficial, even if it is only a five or ten-minute prayer each day. Religion exists as part of what Pierre Bourdieu (1991) called habitus, the overall pattern of life. In cultures where one religion is dominant, the habit of life is shaped to enable most people to participate in the ceremonies – be that time away from work to attend Sunday church services in Christian societies, structured pauses in the working day to pray in Islamic societies, or comparable practices in other cultures. It is equally the case for minority religions (or any religion in highly secular societies such as modern Britain) find themselves on a back foot because the daily habitus of society does not enable their ritual patterns, mostly simply ignoring them but sometimes actively undermining them. The habitus of Ancient Egypt enabled daily life and ritualism to dovetail. Unless the reader is independently wealthy, their time is likely to be at the beck and call of employers (and others) and compromises will have to be made around the kinds of ritual engagement that can be fitted in with all the other commitments of life.

Modern Kemeticism can be understood as a continuance of a process that began with Rome occupying ancient Kemet. The Egyptians themselves never had much interest in proselytising their faith to other parts of the world. What deities the people of Punt, Habeshet, Greece or anywhere else worshipped was of minimal relevance and there was no drive to get the people of foreign lands to leave their deities in favour of the Netjeru. Even when Rome arrived there was still no great interest in that, however the Romans did bring one of the first forms of globalisation. Every land that Rome conquered became part of Rome, with Roman laws, customs, notions of citizenship, dietary preferences, and so forth brought in as a bolt-on to the native culture. Over time it has to be noted that the wealthy and upwardly mobile often took less and less interest in their ancestral cultures in favour of the Roman ways that would smooth their passage towards power and security in the upper echelons of imperial society. Comparable processes can be seen in other large-scale empires over the last two thousand years.

An unusual feature of the early Roman Empire, not often found in more recent empires, was its religious pluralism. Having acquired a new territory not only was there an interest in seeing the various goods that might be exported (including human cargo, unfortunately) but also in the deities and religious notions of the new land – at least those notions that were compatible with pre-existing Roman ones. Polytheism, by its nature, is pluralist – which is to say that it does not see truth as the exclusive possession of any one faith or one perception of divine forces. A person might attend the temple of Father Jupiter one day and pray in the temple of Isis the next with no conflict of conscience or anyone considering them odd. From the Roman stance, incorporating the deities of the new territory was a form of constructive integration of the new populace and a way of demonstrating that the empire had spiritual as well as military dominance. The Romans engaged in the ritual of *invitatio* to welcome the deities of a subject peoples to their own side, offering the grand temples, annual festivities and so forth to make it worth their while.

Modern day polytheists continue this sort of attitude, as do many other people whose spirituality might not be called polytheist but is certainly very pluralist. The issue of spiritual geography has been mentioned quite a few times over the course of this book, and we return to it again here. The people of Kemet centred their faith on their land, their river, their weather, their native animal species, the ritual calendar generated from the patterns of all these factors. Having no interest in spreading the faith to other lands, no thought was put into how someone living a thousand miles away from the Nile and its seasons and creatures might relate to these concepts. It was the Roman decision to build temples to the goddess they called Isis (and others) in far-flung parts of the Empire, rather than a drive by the Egyptians themselves to spread her worship. This is not to say that Egyptian merchants, soldiers, and so forth who washed up in foreign shores did not appreciate having a building in which to honour the Netjeru of their homeland.

So, we return to this question which in many ways is so central to this book – what is the Nile? Is it a river specific to one part of the world, and the spirit of it confined to that geographic region? Will Hapi, divine presence of the Nile, manifest before a pagan prancing round a candle and a cup of tap water in Walthamstow? There are many modern pagans who will swear blind that they have felt the numinous aura of Hapi in Glasgow, Canberra, Madrid, or Maputo. This author for one is not about to refute the validity of their experiences. The nature of these encounters begs a lot of theological questions, such as the extent to which geography means much of anything to transcendent entities. There is an old adage that a hundred years is a long time in America and a hundred miles a long way in Britain. Scale is relative. Perhaps in the physical world a thousand miles seems a vast distance, but in the spirit world it is a journey of moments. Others reading this may feel that actually geography is central and that an entity described as being part of a particular river, mountain, forest or whatever is, indeed, attached to that place and no other. From this perspective a ritual to an entity tied to some place many hundreds of miles away might be akin to a trunk call or a Skype link – better than nothing but rather patchy and ultimately lacking the personal touch of a direct physical presence. Coming from this philosophical stance, a ritualist may decide that the Nile is a concept as much as a stretch of specific water.

If conceptual, the Nile becomes the Great River on which any ancient community depended. The modern world with reservoirs and pumped-in water no longer has this focus on a singular river or lake, and maybe that is part of the reason why we so often take water courses for granted and treat them so shoddily when it comes to pollution. The person living in Glasgow, Canberra, or wherever it may be might opt to focus their ritual and communion on the local river or lake – get to know its spirit and tides and creatures in the same the people of Kemet did with the Nile. The same philosophy may not apply across the board with other Netjeru. Merely because there are no crocodiles living in your locale does not mean that Sobek will not turn up wherever he pleases. Some entities are far more free-roaming than others.

In ancient times many rituals made use of waters from the Nile. In modern, geographically dispersed times it is recommended that the reader use water taken from a suitably clean, unpolluted local river, stream, or lake (in preference to tap or bottled water). Not only will this be more convenient, but it will help reinforce links to the local landscape as well as echoing traditional practices. Do check with the spirit of the waterway that it is willing to participate.

One issue worth reflecting on is the relationship between the modern Kemetic and both ancient and contemporary Egyptian culture and history. Islamic State has engaged in horrific crimes against both people and culture, such as the brutal murder in 2015 of elderly archaeologist Khaled al-Asaad for the "crime" of preserving the polytheist past of Syria, an act roundly condemned by fundamentalists as a form of shirk (a pejorative Arabic word for polytheism), and the destruction of Palmyra. There have been incidents in Egypt with political extremists associated with Islamic State, but the Egyptian government have dealt with them very forcefully – doubtless concerned about the deleterious impact on extremely lucrative tourism. At one point it brought in well over $12 billion to the economy, though this has declined with recent terrorist incidents. Where ancient temples, pyramids, and other buildings or museum exhibits are at risk (be that from human violence, pollution damage, or anything else) do the worldwide devotees of the Netjeru have a moral duty to help out be that financially or in some other manner? Equally, archaeologists are forever seeking financing for digs. If it helps deepen knowledge of the past, ought we help? The same question might be raised with respect to Heathens helping preserve or uncover relics of the Scandinavian and Germanic past, Druids with respect to the cultural history of the Celtic countries, and so forth.

Alexei Kondratiev (1998) raised some interesting points for Druids and others interested in the spiritual practices of Celtic lands that culture is not frozen in an amber sphere of the past. They exist in the present too, albeit in forms that have changed over time. Only small numbers of modern Irish, Welsh, Cornish etc. people are practicing pagans of any description. He reflects on what relationship the modern devotee of Celtic paganism ought to have with non-pagan forms of spirituality tied to those lands – such as Irish Catholicism, the Wee Free Church of Scotland, Welsh chapel and various other expressions. It is not a clear-cut issue, especially when a number of those contemporary manifestations are actively hostile towards paganism and would not welcome involvement. Comparable questions might be raised for Kemetics where almost all modern Egyptians are Muslim. It is easy to focus on a romanticised distant past and ignore modern cultures with all their complexities and political challenges. However, it is equally clear that the preservation of past monuments and relics is heavily reliant on engagement with 21st century people who might regard devotion to the Netjeru (or other deities in other cultures) as bizarre, laughable, or even immoral. Many modern Egyptians are fiercely proud of their antiquities, though not to the point of worshipping the Netjeru. It can also be noted that modern cultures often contain nuggets of the distant past – recipes, music, dances, and other aspects of culture that have defied the passage of time and provide continuity between today and several thousand years ago. Understanding the present helps with learning more about the past.

As well as commitment to places, objects, and people in Egypt there is also what might be termed a diaspora of artefacts in museums and private collections across the world. Statues that might have been objects of devotion two thousand years ago now sit in glass cases as objects of mild curiosity. The Kemetic could seek to establish relationship with sacred statues and other important items displayed in their local museum. Some museums might be willing to accommodate people for whom some of their exhibits hold spiritual significance.

Just as the Greek government has strong views on the matter of the Elgin Marbles being returned to their homeland, so many may have decided opinions on the restoration of Egyptian antiquities to their land of origin – especially where they were acquired by somewhat debatable methods. Some people might wish to campaign for the return of specific items although I suggest this urge to repatriation be balanced with consideration for the ongoing peace and stability of the region. It would be a terrible loss to return some unique work of beauty only for extremists to later blow it to smithereens.

An element of devotion is keeping a tradition alive and fresh. The manner of doing this will likely vary according to skills. Those of a didactic bent could run classes teaching people about Egyptian history or mythology, poets and musicians and storytellers could entertain and inspire, artists create beautiful things using ancient techniques.

Funeral practices have been mentioned earlier, along with the note that a great many of the methods used in times past are now illegal in many countries. For those who commit themselves to one or more of the Netjeru, at some point it will be useful to consider how they wish to adapt the ancient habitus for the dead to their own eventual demise or that of their nearest and dearest. One of the key issues is the preservation of the corpse. In Kemet people sought to preserve the *sah*, the body, feeling this was key to a good afterlife. Some of the chemicals and techniques now commonly used in embalming have been shown to cause environmental problems, which needs consideration. The Kemetic may want to reflect on what they feel happens in the afterlife if the body is either cremated or left to rot away naturally. Whatever the answer, it will have some impact on decisions made about arranging for funerals. Under British law (the reader needs to check for other legal systems if they live in a different part of the world) it is possible, indeed advisable, to appoint an Executor for one's funeral who is a distinct person from the Executor for financial arrangements. The funeral executor is empowered by the testament to carry out the reader's wishes, provided they are legal ones. This could be as simple as a decision about cremation or burial through to more complex arrangements involving preferences around embalming, styles of coffin, grave goods, music, and all the rest of it. If it is likely that the relatives or friends who outlive the person reading this book will not understand Kemetic beliefs and ceremonies, then the guidelines left in his or her Will may serve as a great relief to them in knowing that they are doing what would have been wanted. This codicil can also leave a small amount of money to pay for the funeral arrangements and give instructions about the disposal of ritual objects, books that might well only appeal to a fellow Kemetic, robes, and so forth. If the reader opts for burial, it may be possible to have some ceremonial regalia interred in the coffin, depending on the rules and regulations of the cemetery.

Potentially these could be applied to pets at the end of their lives, where there may be a wider range of legal possibilities – though the cost of getting a cat mummified might well prove prohibitive. In the UK people who own their homes outright can have, water tables and public safety permitting, up to two bodies legally interred on their premises – I refer to legitimate funerals here, not serial killers sticking their neighbours under the patio. If one of these graves were the reader's own, then they could make arrangements to have past pets placed in with them or at least adjacent to their own plot. It is, of course, worth noting that the act of turning a garden into a burial ground immediately plummets the resale value of the property. It is also making the land of scant value to developers, which is an added reason to do it. In 1851 William Mackenzie was buried in a Liverpool graveyard with a 15-foot pyramid as a marker above him. The churchyard at Brightling, East Sussex contains a 25-foot pyramid sited over the graves of Mad Jack Fuller and his two wives. Whether any of these people had an especial passion for Egyptian culture or mysticism is unknown, but it does open up a realm of possible funeral practices – for those with sufficient means – that could bewilder future generations.

Renenutet, the snake goddess who distributes sacred names, was sometimes considered to be the consort of Shai, the Netjer who oversees the concept named after him. In later Egyptian artwork he was sometimes shown with a cobra head rather than the more conventionally human form of earlier art. One of the functions of this god is to measure out the lifespan. This raises some interesting questions about Kemetic perceptions of destiny and the degree of control we mortals have over it. For example, if Shai measures out a person's life as being 90 years, is it possible for that to be altered or is it a fixed quantity? Would the person be able to defy fate by committing suicide at an earlier age, or would some third party with murderous intent be able to change the predestined time span?

People can impact their own lifespan by less dramatic means than suicide, such as through abusing toxic substances. Doubtless many readers will know of someone who chain-smoked or drank like a fish but inexplicably lived to a ripe old age, outliving many others whose overindulgences were significantly less. Genetic factors undoubtedly play a role here in who succumbs quickly and who lurches on as a creaking gate seemingly forever. Perhaps Shai can be understood as the deity who sets such biological parameters.

The moralistic poem 'Dispute between a Man and His Ba' has been mentioned previously, and it is made clear by the ethereal *ba* that the unhappy poet who wishes to kill himself should not do so because the date of his death is set by the gods. He must die on the predestined date and not attempt to hurry his exit from the world along. Unfortunately, the final verses of the poem are lost, so it is no longer known if the poet follows his *ba's* advice or commits suicide despite it.

The word *shai* is often translated as meaning fate or destiny. Other curious moral and philosophical questions arise with this issue of the setting of death dates. If the 90-year old meets her end on a plane crash that kills a dozen other people, do we consider the crashing of that plane to be somehow predestined and something for which pilot error cannot be held accountable or, if the crash were caused by a terrorist bomb, were the political extremists in some bizarre sense destined to do what they did and so not fully culpable? A number of religions have preached a doctrine of predestination and run into the same moral conundrums. Where the 90-year old dies peacefully in bed there is little issue to task over, but where their demise is down to the morally reprehensible actions of others then we are faced with a situation in which those people seem little more than the glove puppets of cosmic forces and so denied any notion of culpability or personal choice. Whilst it is a notion that some people are comfortable with, it does go against the grain of much philosophical thought and the wish to perceive ourselves and others are mostly free agents who choose whether or not to commit egregious deeds.

A middle road is to suggest that *shai* flows in harmony with *ma'at*, the wood grain of the universe, but that disruptive beings (human or otherwise) can cause disharmony by seeking to divert the flow of what is meant to be. Nonetheless the pattern of the universe seeks to re-establish itself wherever it can. A popular notion from quantum physics which has been woven into a hundred films, novels, and TV shows is that each choice we make creates alternative parallel universes. In this dimension JFK died in 1963 but there will be another dimension in which he dodged the bullet and lived longer and so the course of history goes differently there. Given that there are over seven billion humans making decisions every minute of every day, the number of alternate universes would be astronomical. It is hard to consider that my decision whether to have a cup of tea or a cup of coffee creates two separate realities. Perhaps the vast majority of our decisions are of so trivial a nature that they make no real difference to anything and do not fracture universes into endless parallels. The universe flows on regardless, like a river momentarily flowing around a pebble dropped into before continuing on its merry way. It is a salutary thought that most of what we say and do and think just does not matter a damn in the greater scheme – and the philosophy of *ma'at* does suggest that there is definitely a scheme of some kind unfurling itself.

Certain major acts may disrupt the pattern irretrievably, but the majority of *isfet* deeds cause small ripples that are ultimately smoothed out. If Susan is destined to do something but is killed before she can complete the task, the force of *ma'at* simply finds someone else to get the job done. In this sense *shai* becomes less a grandiose destiny for us alone – the kind of thing beloved of fantasy novelists – and more akin to a stage in a relay race. If we drop that baton, someone else will pick it up. Our part in the race may be over, but the match continues on regardless because we individual runners are not, ultimately, all that important. As a concept it is a useful antidote to egomania.

The word *shai* also means pig. The early Egyptians did not seem particularly interested in this linkage of words. It was not until the Greek occupation that images of the god Shai started to appear with a pig head or as a pig with a snake head. If the reader fancies milking that imagery for all it is worth, consider that the philosophy of *shai* leads us to be less pig-headed about our own importance, instead filling our heads with the wisdom of the serpent.

The word *shai* appears in past-tense form in a hymn to Amun which declares that the god, "*gives more than that which is fated to him whom He loves*". This could simply be a rather generic usage of the word, but may allude to the sense of *shai* being a kind of minimalist sketch of that which is meant to be with plenty of room for deities or mortals to pad out or alter the sketch. Following this idea, the *shai* distributed by Shai at the birth of a child may be their small portion of the cosmic *ma'at*, the part of a wider pattern which they should strive to achieve but which also leaves plenty of room for innovation in life and freedom of choice. It should also be thought of as more akin to the Greek idea of *telos*, a goal to strive for rather than a heavy burden that must be carried lest terrible consequence result from failure. What we fall short of or simply die before achieving, the cosmos will delegate to others.

Chapter Ten

Quo Vadis?

What you do next will vary according to whether you are an absolute newcomer to the Kemetic tradition or a long-term practitioner. A novitiate at the beginning of their journey might wish to consider joining a group or finding a teacher who can guide them safely on their travels. Working with others always involves some degree of compromise, which is seldom popular in our highly individualistic era where social media elevates cantankerousness to a virtue, but also gives like minds to compare experiences with, people to keep up motivated and disciplined in spiritual practice, and friendship. The latter is not to be underestimated nor considered as something for which virtual reality contacts can ever be a substitute. The Greek philosophers believed good friendship to be one of the true joys in life, and they knew what they were talking about.

Wanting a network and finding one are two different things. Having just this minute complained about social media, the flip side is that it may well help the novice to track down fellow devotees in their area. If it is at all possible, aim to meet people in person as this will enable a better understanding of their character and the depth of their knowledge than can be had in the virtual world.

Whilst the network of mentors, friends, and fellow devotees is being built up in both the virtual and actual worlds the key advice (unsurprisingly from an author) is – read, read, read! Devote yourself to the temples of Seshet and raid both the public libraries and bookshops so you can learn more of the mythology, history, culture, language, religious customs and so forth. The experienced Kemetic who is reading this book will doubtless already have spent years doing exactly that, but there are always new books, obscure old books, curious websites and so forth that are worth excavating. Alongside reading, honour Tehuti by scribing, or more specifically by journaling. Dreams, visionary experiences, gems of knowledge, questions that will one may get answered, and other milestones along the way are worth jotting down so the reader can revisit their own thoughts, impressions, and discoveries in the years to come.

Whether opting to work alone or in a group, a sensible step to take is the creation of an altar. The exact nature of this will vary according to the kind of environment the reader lives in and could range from a small arrangement on a shelf to an entire room or area of the garden given over to sacred space. Those who share their homes with unsympathetic people, or perhaps live in countries where their neighbours or their government might react with oppressive violence to unusual religious manifestations, could opt for a box or lockable chest that contains their sacred paraphernalia to be brought out or hidden away as the need requires.

In terms of what goes on the altar there is a lot of room for innovation. A focal point would be a statue or painting of the primary deity towards whom the altar is focused and a *kar*, lockable box, in which it can find peace when not being reverenced. When first starting out on the path the reader may not have a particular deity to whom they are drawn, in which case some artwork that captures the interest for aesthetic reasons and shows a selection of Netjeru is appropriate.

Other suitable items include candles, a jug or other container for water and one for scented oils, a jar of natron, a box or jar to keep granular incense dry and another for the charcoal discs. As mentioned elsewhere, reproduction canopic jars can serve this function admirably well. A thurible or other heat-resistant incense burner is useful (unless you are obliged to hide your faith for personal safety, in which case substitute an oil diffuser whose presence and aroma will not arose suspicion). If the reader can safely burn incense or joss sticks, a popular device in ancient times was a burner shaped like the hieroglyph *derep* which takes the form of an outstretched arm with an open palm (the resin or joss sticks being burnt in the cupped palm) and was mentioned in an earlier chapter. Jars of incense and scented oils often had lids in the shape of cat heads, which Michel Malaise (1993) suggests may have been because the goddess Bast was the mother (and so the metaphorical containing womb) of Nefertem the Netjer of perfume. This information might influence the reader's choice of container for oils or resins. A platter for food and other offerings is always useful. These are mostly fairly generic objects that might be found on the altar of pretty much any religion, though they can be tailored by selecting items with an Egyptian design.

More culturally specific items could include an ankh both as an aide memoir to the potency of a well-lived life and also as an item that may be used to inscribe blessings over food, people, or anything else. A sistrum can be used to generate a rhythmic monotone that helps induce trance states. The various tools described in the ritual for the Opening of the Mouth could also be included. The author's altar includes a reproduction *khopesh* (sword with a hooked blade) though in all honesty it has never been used as anything other than a rather striking ornament. In populating an altar, it is wiser to focus on items for which there is a practical use rather than splurging on any and every Egyptian item to which hands can be laid, most of which will just end up gathering dust.

The primary purpose of an altar is to be a focal point for *dua*, reverence. A person does not actually need an altar to worship, but having one provides a visual reminder and also gathers objects that will acquire their own *sekhem* through regular use. In the Egyptian context *sekhem* is the innate power emanating from beings that have animating spirit. This not only includes living humans but at least some dead ones, and most if not all animals, plants, and en-souled forces (such as the Nile itself). This force was not quite understood in the way that Patrick Ziegler interprets it as a healing force. Whilst it certainly can heal, it can also be harnessed in other ways. *Sekhem* is the power to instigate change and can be exerted not only in mystical, ritualistic ways but also in quite prosaic forms such as when a pharaoh gave an order and everyone jumped to.

Developing and reflecting upon one's own *sekhem* is an important step to take. There are many different forms of power and ways to exert it – some good, some bad, many morally indifferent. The journal can be useful here as a way of tracking the sorts of power we each exert to make things happen in the world. This includes everything from using technology to friendly persuasion, using sexual allure, rational argument, threats and menaces, outright violence, casting a vote, bribery, offering trade, using magic, and a thousand other means. The chances are the reader will get used to using certain methods with certain people, in part because we learn what works and humans are pragmatic beasts. There are also situations in which we consciously restrict the methods we use. Threats of violence to get what is wanted undoubtedly work, but the majority of people shy away from using them because they are harmful to good relationships and society in general, and very few people want to turn into that kind of brutal monster. So, dear reader, reflect not only upon the ways you do exert your *sekhem*, but also think about the ways you would prefer to avoid. As Aristotle said, we become what we repeatedly do.

Sociologists use the term agency to describe the exercise of free choice, which *sekhem* is to some extent, but it is primarily the ability to successfully exert one's Will. As a simple example of this, suppose I wanted a cup of tea (I'm English, I always want a cup of tea). I can walk to the kitchen and operate the kettle. This is a successful application of my power to make the things that I want happen. Like so many situations it is contingent on prior exertions of power, such as the past decision to buy a kettle, the acquisition of the knowledge about how to use it (and that vital issue of whether the milk should go in the cup first or second). Were I paralysed from the neck down then the ability to make tea in this fashion would not be possible, at least not without the use of some very impressive and expensive technology. However, I could ask a friend or carer to make tea for me which would still be an exertion of power to get things done. If I were homeless and did not have a kettle, then I could acquire tea by buying it should I be able to get the money through cash-in-hand work, begging, or however else. Possibly I could use strange, mystical powers to produce a cup of tea, but *sekhem* includes all these rather mundane ways of flexing my power as well as the Harry Potter style of making things happen.

Many readers will be interested in developing the more magical expressions of power. There is always something of a risk to gaining a greater sense of one's own power in that it becomes tempting to misuse the newfound abilities – sometimes to abuse other people or indulge petty desires for revenge, but more often through the kind of sheer arrogance that comes with thinking of oneself as terribly important and of others as minions to be ordered about.

In the ancient world temples were usually devoted to one or two deities per shrine, and the clergy centred their reverence upon those. This is not to say that they did not also offer *dua*, devotion, to other Netjeru or attend celebrations at other temples, only that they had a primary focus. This sort of practice is also quite common in modern forms of polytheism, and the newcomer to Kemeticism might wish to establish a particular relationship. It is advised that the reader need not rush into any such communion but should take time to learn about many different gods and see what kind of links build up. If one particular netjer calls to the reader in due course then a formal and private ritual to seal the relationship could be conducted. It is not always obvious why deities choose the people that they do. This author has known of cases where there is an obvious shared interest, such as warrior's deity bonding with a soldier. However, there are other cases where it is harder to comprehend, such as a very bombastic and bullish person taken under the wing of a deity of compassion and gentleness. Perhaps in such situations it is the very absence of certain traits that draws a god or goddess to want to teach them to grow in new directions. The key issue is not to make assumptions – a doctor or nurse might assume they will have the patronage of a healing Netjer and they may well get it, but equally it could be an entirely different deity who takes an interest for reasons which the devotee will not necessarily understand at first.

The philosophy of the *ren* has been discussed at some length, and learning the name of one's own soul is a major part of spiritual development. No nice, easy five-step programme of meditation can be recommended to speed this discovery up. It might take many years of quiet reflection, visionary questing, and other experiences to reveal that name. Having found it, there will (in theory) arise a clearer understanding of one's purpose in life, one's *ma'at* or harmonious place within the world. Knowledge of the *ren* was also linked to having a deep influence over that being, either to aid them through healing or to potentially harm them. Knowing your own *ren* could be an essential tool for self-healing.

The task of discovering the secret name could sensibly be begun by conducting a ritual to contact the serpent goddess Renenutet, offer gifts to her – as the Romans were fond of saying during ritual offerings, *do ut des* (I give that you may give) and even the Bible echoes in Luke 6:38. Like any relationship, links to the divine take a while to build up and to get ourselves in a sufficiently receptive state to understand what is being said. Regular contact over a period of time may help progress towards a revelation. Just be very careful who you share the information with once you have it.

A speculation that interests this author is the question of whether a *ren* remains constant over the course of multiple reincarnations. Once a spirit name is spoken does it echo through any number of bodies that it may inhabit and thus the part it plays in the unfurling *ma'at* of the world remains consistent over the passage of many lives? I like to think that it does, but perhaps that is more romanticism on my part than any profound insight into the nature of the universe.

Earlier in chapter five mention was made of the term hotepian, as an insult used by some Black Nationalists in America to goad other Nationalists (for whom the word *hotep* is a form of greeting and mutual recognition) whom they see as too patriarchal and macho. This movement strikes the author as little more than yet another form of racial supremacism, as misguided, belligerent, and short-sighted as any other. It is a shame the word *hotep* has become caught up in an intersectionality feud. Divisive politics to one side, *hotep* can be understood as a philosophical concept. The word has a number of layered meanings, including the state of peace, the injunction to be at peace, a ceremonial offering, contentment, and a general sense of being in keeping with the patterns of *ma'at*. A derived word in the Coptic language also means reconciliation.

This interflow of meanings has strong resemblance to the Lithuanian word *darna*, a philosophical concept within the Romuvan religion. This term also means peace, carrying with it the belief that a person must begin by coming to terms with themselves and finding a peaceful acceptance in their soul. From here they can be in peaceful harmony with immediate family (which includes any pets, farm animals, trees in the garden etc.), from there peace with extended family and neighbours. Onward and outward the circles of care ripple as the power of *darna* enables people to come to good terms with wider and wider numbers of living beings. There are connections to the Vedic idea of dharma and, it can readily be seen, to the Egyptian *hotep*. The familial resemblance between these words does not make them interchangeable, because each has its own subtle nuances which may not be shared by related terms.

An example of a nuance in *hotep* is the meaning of an offering made to the Netjeru, ancestors, or others. To establish peace with another person (in the broad sense of that word) becomes an act of offering, the furthering of *ma'at* being as much a gift to the gods as incense, wine, or any of the more usual sacrifices. A sacrifice is not only an object made sacred by the giving but also something that involves a cost or effort to the giver (somebody has to buy the wine or make the incense, after all). The act of creating peace and harmony can often involve considerable effort, especially if we consider the Coptic understanding of reconciling with some person or group with whom there has previously been bad feeling or injury. The act of bringing something into being is referred to as *seheper*, a function of any devotee of the Netjer is to being *ma'at* into being.

This is a general reminder that gifts to the deities are not only those things offered within a highly ritualistic context. Writing a book can be a gift to Seshet, volunteering at the cat shelter may be very appreciated by Bast, supporting a pregnant woman who is struggling may get the thumbs up from Tuaret. So too making peace, spreading order and harmony sits well with Ma'at and, indeed, all the Netjeru.

When considering those big philosophical questions about the meaning and purpose of life, a good and practical place to start is to consider how to attain greater *hotep* in relationships. The reader could think of the various people in their life and pick one with which to begin, creating a more balanced, peaceful, contented relationship. One by one work on spreading the sense of harmony, treating the amount of effort required to improve relationships as an offering to the Netjeru. There will inevitably be times when the efforts fall on stony ground because the other person is simply not interested in improving the situation, but at least the attempt will be a form of offering. One of the texts mentioned several times earlier in this book, the Instructions of Ptahhotep, can be read as a good guideline on what constitutes a harmonious relationship. Some of the views expressed there are reflective of the gender politics of the day and may not be too well received by some people in the 21st century, so it should be treated as a guideline rather than a Divine Command. For example, he warns against getting too friendly with the women of a house that is being visited and also advises husbands not to allow their wives to dominate the marriage.

In the poem about the argument between the Man and his Ba, the unhappy man recites many verses about how awful the world is. The various conditions that he cites, such as the greed and dishonesty of his neighbours and the duplicitous and treacherous nature of his so-called friends, are a litany of *isfet* in action. He looks upon the world and sees an absence of *ma'at* without an ounce of *hotep* to be found anywhere. A great many people probably open a newspaper or turn on the TV news and feel much the same, that there is more misery and wickedness in the world than we know how to cope with. There is plenty of goodness in the world too, but it is easy for it to become overshadowed by the shoddy nature of people at times.

If the reader opts to create a habitus of daily (or weekly, or however frequent) ritual then an eminently useful topic for the meditative act would be to reflect on what could be done that day or week to make the world a better place, to foster *hotep* in word and deed. Rather than dwelling on what is wrong with the world, like the despairing poet, focus on what good can be done to counter it.

From here on, may you enjoy following the paw prints of the jackals in the sand as they lead you to oases in the desert.

Recommended Reading

Asante, Molefi (2015), *African Pyramids of Knowledge: Kemet, Afrocentricity and Africology*. Universal Write Publications LLC

Assmann, Jan (2002), *The Mind of Egypt: History and Meaning in the Time of the Pharaohs*. Metropolitan Books

Bourghouts, J F (1978), *Ancient Egyptian Magical Texts*. Brill, Leiden

David, Rosalie (2002), *Religion and Magic in Ancient Egypt*. Penguin Books

De Vartavan, Christian (2016), *Vocalised Dictionary of Ancient Egypt*. SAIS, London

Diop, Cheik Anta (1988), *Precolonial Black Africa*. Chicago Review Press

Dunand, Francoise & Zivie-Coche, Christiane (2004), *Gods and Men in Egypt 3000 BCE to 395 CE*. Cornell Paperbacks

Erman, Adolf (author) and Blackman, Aylward (translator) (1995), *Ancient Egyptian Poetry and Prose*. Dover Publications, New York.

Graves-Brown, Carolyn (2010), *Dancing for Hathor, Women in Ancient Egypt*. Bloomsbury Academic

John, Billie Walker (2003), *The Setian*. Ignotus Press

Kaster, Joseph (1995), *The Wisdom of Ancient Egypt*. Michael O'Mara Books Limited

Kemboly, Mpay. 2010. *The Question of Evil in Ancient Egypt*. London: Golden House Publications

Lichtim, Miriam (1975), *Ancient Egyptian Literature Volume 1: The Old and Middle Kingdoms*. University of California Press

Mourad, Anna-Latifa (2015), *Rise of the Hyksos*. Archaeopress Publishing Ltd

Pinch, Geraldine (2006), *Magic in Ancient Egypt*. The British Museum Press

Rautman, Alison E. (2000), *Reading the Body*. University of Pennsylvania Press

Journal Articles

Baumgarten, A., Assmann, J., Stroumsa, G. G. (Hg.), "Self, Soul and Body" (Studies in the history of religions 78), Leiden 1998, S. 384-403

Harrell, James. "Gemstones". *UCLA Encyclopedia of Egyptology*, 2012

Jonckheere, Frans. "L'Eunuque dans l'Égypte pharaonique". *Revue d'Histoire des Sciences*, vol. 7, No. 2 (April-June 1954), pp. 139-155

Moret, Alexandre. "Le rituel du culte divin". *Journalier en Egypte*, 1902, Paris

Ottens, Sandra. "The Seven Hathors, Musicians of fate". Leiden, 2012

Pouls Wegner, Mary-Ann. "Wepwawet in Context: a reconsideration of the jackal deity and its role in the spatial organisation of the North Abydos landscape"

Reeder, Greg. "A Rite of Passage: The Enigmatic Tekenu in Ancient Egyptian Funerary Ritual". *KMT: A Modern Journal of Ancient Egypt*, autumn 1994, vol.5 no.3

Shaltout, Mosalam & Belmonte, Juan Antonio. "On the Orientation of Ancient Egyptian Temples I: Upper Egypt and Lower Nubia". 2005

Van Loon, A J. "Law and order in Ancient Egypt". 2014, Leiden University.

Zecchi, Marco. "Sobek of Shedet. The Crocodile God in the Fayyum in the Dynastic Period". 2010

MOON BOOKS

PAGANISM & SHAMANISM

What is Paganism? A religion, a spirituality, an alternative belief system, nature worship? You can find support for all these definitions (and many more) in dictionaries, encyclopaedias, and text books of religion, but subscribe to any one and the truth will evade you. Above all Paganism is a creative pursuit, an encounter with reality, an exploration of meaning and an expression of the soul. Druids, Heathens, Wiccans and others, all contribute their insights and literary riches to the Pagan tradition. Moon Books invites you to begin or to deepen your own encounter, right here, right now. If you have enjoyed this book, why not tell other readers by posting a review on your preferred book site.

Recent bestsellers from Moon Books are:

Journey to the Dark Goddess
How to Return to Your Soul
Jane Meredith
Discover the powerful secrets of the Dark Goddess and
transform your depression, grief and pain into healing
and integration.
Paperback: 978-1-84694-677-6 ebook: 978-1-78099-223-5

Shamanic Reiki
Expanded Ways of Working with Universal Life Force Energy
Llyn Roberts, Robert Levy
Shamanism and Reiki are each powerful ways of healing; together,
their power multiplies. *Shamanic Reiki* introduces techniques to
help healers and Reiki practitioners tap ancient healing wisdom.
Paperback: 978-1-84694-037-8 ebook: 978-1-84694-650-9

Pagan Portals – The Awen Alone
Walking the Path of the Solitary Druid
Joanna van der Hoeven
An introductory guide for the solitary Druid, *The Awen Alone* will
accompany you as you explore, and seek out your own place
within the natural world.
Paperback: 978-1-78279-547-6 ebook: 978-1-78279-546-9

A Kitchen Witch's World of Magical Herbs & Plants
Rachel Patterson
A journey into the magical world of herbs and plants, filled with
magical uses, folklore, history and practical magic. By popular
writer, blogger and kitchen witch, Tansy Firedragon.
Paperback: 978-1-78279-621-3 ebook: 978-1-78279-620-6

Medicine for the Soul
The Complete Book of Shamanic Healing
Ross Heaven
All you will ever need to know about shamanic healing and how to
become your own shaman...
Paperback: 978-1-78099-419-2 ebook: 978-1-78099-420-8

Shaman Pathways – The Druid Shaman
Exploring the Celtic Otherworld
Danu Forest
A practical guide to Celtic shamanism with exercises and
techniques as well as traditional lore for exploring the Celtic
Otherworld.
Paperback: 978-1-78099-615-8 ebook: 978-1-78099-616-5

Traditional Witchcraft for the Woods and Forests
A Witch's Guide to the Woodland with Guided Meditations and
Pathworking
Mélusine Draco
A Witch's guide to walking alone in the woods, with guided
meditations and pathworking.
Paperback: 978-1-84694-803-9 ebook: 978-1-84694-804-6

Naming the Goddess
Trevor Greenfield
Naming the Goddess is written by over eighty adherents and
scholars of Goddess and Goddess Spirituality.
Paperback: 978-1-78279-476-9 ebook: 978-1-78279-475-2

Shapeshifting into Higher Consciousness
Heal and Transform Yourself and Our World with Ancient
Shamanic and Modern Methods
Llyn Roberts
Ancient and modern methods that you can use every day to
transform yourself and make a positive difference in the world.
Paperback: 978-1-84694-843-5 ebook: 978-1-84694-844-2

Readers of ebooks can buy or view any of these bestsellers by
clicking on the live link in the title. Most titles are published in
paperback and as an ebook. Paperbacks are available in traditional
bookshops. Both print and ebook formats are available online.

Find more titles and sign up to our readers' newsletter at
http://www.johnhuntpublishing.com/paganism
Follow us on Facebook at https://www.facebook.com/MoonBooks
and Twitter at https://twitter.com/MoonBooksJHP